Conquering *the* Fear *of* Failure

Conquering *the* Fear *of* Failure

Lessons from the
Life of Joshua

ERWIN W. LUTZER

Kregel
Publications

Conquering the Fear of Failure: Lessons from the Life of Joshua
© 2002, 2011 by Erwin Lutzer

Published by Kregel Publications, a division of Kregel, Inc.,
P.O. Box 2607, Grand Rapids, MI 49501.

All Scripture quotations, unless otherwise indicated, are from
the NEW AMERICAN STANDARD BIBLE®. Copyright ©
1960, 1962, 1963, 1968, 1971, 1972, 1973, 1975, 1977 by The
Lockman Foundation. Used by permission. (www.Lockman
.org)

Scripture quotations marked KJV are from the King James
Version.

Scripture quotations marked NKJV are from the New King
James Version. Copyright © 1982 by Thomas Nelson, Inc. Used
by permission. All rights reserved.

Library of Congress Cataloging-in-Publication Data
Lutzer, Erwin W.
    Conquering the fear of failure / Erwin Lutzer.
      p. cm.
    1. Christian life—Biblical teaching. 2. Failure
(Psychology)—Religious aspects—Christianity. 3. Bible.
O.T. Joshua—Criticism, interpretation, etc. I. Title.
BS680.C47 L88   2001   222'.2'06—dc21   2001005824

ISBN 978-0-8254-3905-6

Printed in the United States of America

11 12 13 14 15 / 5 4 3 2 1

To Fred Hickman,
my father-in-law,
whose submission to God's sovereignty
has enabled him to overcome the obstacles of life.

Contents

Introduction / 9

1. The Grasshopper Complex / 13
2. When Faith Doesn't Work / 27
3. Listening to the Right Voice / 41
4. A Winning Strategy / 53
5. Taking the First Step / 67
6. Getting Ready for Battle / 77
7. Your First Big Fight / 89
8. The High Cost of Hidden Sin / 101
9. Taking Charge Over the Enemy / 113
10. Living With a Bad Decision / 127
11. The Power of Prayer / 137
12. Overcoming Obstacles / 147
13. Making the Promises Work / 159
14. Choosing God / 171

Introduction

A woman asked her pastor, "Do you think we ought to pray for even the little things of life?" He replied, "Can you think of *anything* in your life that is big to God?"

All of our problems, whether great or small, are of equal concern to God; nothing seems either too little or too big to Him. To an Olympic champion, it makes little difference whether he is asked to carry one feather or ten.

Isaiah pointed out that the God who created the sun and stars is also quite capable of keeping them all under control. " 'To whom then will you liken Me that I should be his equal?' says the Holy One. Lift up your eyes on high and see who has created these stars, the One who leads forth their host by number, He calls them all by name; because of the greatness of His might and the strength of His power not one of them is missing" (Is 40:25-26).

That God is all-powerful is generally accepted by all Christians. But how do we access this potential so that we can live an authentic Christian life?

God is willing to help free us from slavery to sin and emotional distress. The dilemma that confronts us is: Why in the face of all His promises do we fare so badly? Why are so many of us slaves to various addictions, living with broken relationships, or quite simply defeated at every turn in our spiritual pilgrimage? Why?

In our disappointment we might conclude that God has actually promised too much. Read a passage such as the Upper Room Discourse (John 13–17) and meditate on what Christ told His disciples. He assured them that they had no need for fear, they would receive supernatural peace, and the Holy Spirit would come to indwell them. And whatever they asked, God would do.

In sharp contrast to such incredible claims, we face a whole litany of personal and corporate defeats within the believing church. The gap between God's promises and our performance seems incredibly wide. Has God "oversold" Himself?

Another possibility is that we have not had enough instruction on how God's promises are to be applied. We may expect Him to give us everything we ask for, forgetting that there are some tough requirements for experiencing the blessing of God.

This is why we must return to the Book of Joshua. More than any other book, Joshua teaches what it takes *from us* to see the promises of God fulfilled. On the one hand God told Joshua with clarity that the land of Canaan was his; on the other hand he had to expend blood, sweat, and tears to claim his inheritance.

The Book of Joshua is largely a history of wars. No sooner did the Israelites enter the land than the Canaanites dug in for battle. Every step they claimed had to be wrested from angry foes. There was no such thing as an uncontested victory.

Likewise for us, to take the promises of God seriously is to declare war on the world, the flesh, and the devil. The minute we begin to seek God's blessings, the forces of evil come out of hiding.

We might spare ourselves disappointment with God if we remember that He did not fulfill His word to Joshua in a single day. In fact, waiting for God to fulfill His Word is not an exception but the rule. God gave promises to Abraham that he did not live to see fulfilled. God's Word is completely trustworthy, but we must be willing to wait.

We shall learn that Joshua's path to victory was uneven, fraught with setbacks and bitter disappointments. Joshua himself made mistakes; and at times his people rebelled and had to retreat from territory that was within their grasp. When Joshua died the war was not over. There were still pockets of resistance that continued to harass the Israelites.

The purpose of this book is to help us grasp principles for applying God's promises. With the Bible in one hand and our awareness of the inconsistencies of human nature in the other, we can hopefully *close the gap between promises and performance.*

Conquering the Fear of Failure is not a commentary on Joshua (many excellent ones already exist). Nor is it primarily devotional in nature. Rather, it is a handbook guiding us through the pitfalls of spiritual growth, capturing territory from Satan and using it for the glory of God.

To profit most from this book, read the passage of Scripture cited at the beginning of each chapter.

My prayer is that through studying Joshua we all will take one more giant step toward spiritual maturity. In the process we shall discover that God is all-powerful and worthy of our trust.

Chapter One

The Grasshopper Complex
(Read Numbers 13:25-33)

Personality disorders have become a fact of life. Everyone, Christian and non-Christian alike, seems to have one complex or another. Some of us are introverts; some extroverts. Others may suffer from paranoia or schizophrenia.

But there is one complex that might be the most prevalent of all: *the Grasshopper Complex.* And no other disorder can so paralyze our spiritual walk with God.

Twelve spies had gone into the land of Canaan to determine the military strategy needed to conquer this Promised Land. Ten were intimidated by the project, believing that the inhabitants were too well fortified to be uprooted.

Specifically, the majority said, "We are not able to go up against the people, for they are too strong for us" (Nm 13:31). They gave a bad report, causing thousands who heard their story to tremble in fear.

Two of the men, Joshua and Caleb, quieted the people and begged to differ with their peers. They said, "We should by all means go up and take possession of it, for we shall surely overcome it" (13:30).

But the majority report prevailed (see Nm 14:1-4) as the ten spies convincingly exaggerated the difficulty of obeying God.

"The land through which we have gone, in spying it out, is a land that devours its inhabitants; and all the people whom we saw in it are men of great size. There also we saw the Nephilim (the sons of Anak are part of the Nephilim); and we became like grasshoppers in our own sight, and so we were in their sight" (13:32-33).

Notice: the ten spies saw the Canaanites as *giants* and themselves as *grasshoppers.* How easily a giant can crush a grasshopper!

There are several powerful reasons why the whole nation of Israel adopted the Grasshopper Complex:

First, the Canaanites were better armed. Whereas Israel had but a few staves, the pagans they were supposed to conquer had horses and chariots and had mastered the use of iron. Militarily, there was great disparity between the two antagonists. The Canaanite armies were well trained and practiced in war. For centuries they had fought among themselves and had mastered the art of cruelty. Their strong organization and superior weapons made them formidable.

Second, the Canaanites lived in walled cities, while the Israelites lived in tents. In war there is a vast difference between defending a fortification and wresting it from the enemy. Only a few soldiers are needed to defend a walled city; but it usually takes a hundred times that number to actually capture it.

Quite literally, the Israelites had no place to hide. No foxholes; no fortifications. They were hard-pressed to think of a single advantage they would have in an all-out war.

Third, the Canaanites were bigger physically. Yes, there were giants in the land. Why the Canaanites were taller we don't know, but they had in fact developed into a physically superior race and the Israelites paled in comparison.

Looked at in one way, it made sense for the people to choose the majority report. Everything was stacked against them. Why risk almost certain death when you have the option of staying in the wilderness to be fed by God?

The one factor that could have significantly changed the equation was that God was on the side of the Israelites. More than that, the Almighty had given a specific promise that if they would believe Him for victory, they would achieve it. Simple faith in God would shift the military balance of power. For who can stand against the armies of the Almighty?

But *it is always easier to see giants than to see God.* In the presence of powerful enemies, we tend to revise downward our estimate of God's faithfulness and power.

We adopt the Grasshopper Complex whenever we *turn away from a God-given challenge for fear that we lack the resources to tackle it,* or when we try to avoid facing a problem that is hindering our spiritual progress.

Recently I spoke to a woman who could not complete a résumé for a job without hearing a voice that told her she would be a failure. A man I know was reared in a home where nothing was ever good enough for his father. The son is now haunted with the feeling that he is a disappointment to everyone, including God. He is, he says, "doomed to fail." The Grasshopper Complex.

The ten spies caught a bad case of the Grasshopper Complex, and the virus spread to the whole multitude. Moses wanted a simple report of the good land that was to be conquered. What he got was the fruit of fear—the destructive influence of a bad example.

What are some characteristics of the Grasshopper Complex?

A Doubting Heart

The vocal majority of the Israelite spies could think only of the many reasons why they would lose in battle; they could think of no reasons why they might win. Though God had given them a promise, it seemed unrealistic so they did not believe it. "We are not able to go up against the people, for they are too strong for us" (Nm 13:31).

Why all this negativism? Perhaps they thought God had failed them in the past. They remembered the bitter waters of Marah more clearly than the sweet waters that eventually flowed from that oasis. They recalled that God had let them go thirsty until Moses was asked to smite the rock in Horeb. Then there was the war with Amalek, and later the terrifying day in which three thousand Israelites were killed by the Levites because of the golden calf.

Even more vivid in their memories may have been the recent dispute over their "menu" in the desert. They had grown weary of manna and complained because they did not have meat. God punished them by granting their request but combining it with judgment (see Nm 11:33).

How could they trust a God who had dealt with them so severely? What if He were to turn against them in the middle of their battle against the Canaanites? To trust an invisible God to fight a very visible army was asking a bit much. Furthermore, they were in no mood to fight.

Though we might be tempted to excuse their unbelief, God was not quite so sympathetic. He took their decision as a personal referendum on His credibility. Though He forgave their sin in response to Moses' prayer, He was *very* angry: "How long shall I bear with this evil congregation who are grumbling against Me? I have heard the complaints of the sons of Israel, which they are making against Me.... Your corpses shall fall in this wilderness, even all your numbered men, according to your complete number from twenty years old and upward, who have grumbled against Me" (Nm 14:27, 29).

God attributed the Israelites' fear of failure to their hard hearts. He was angry with that whole generation and swore that they would not enter the land. The author of the Book of Hebrews recites this story and warns, "Take care, brethren, lest there should be in any one of you an evil, unbelieving heart, in falling away from the living God" (Heb 3:12).

A doubting heart is not just a minor fault that can be overlooked as one failing among many. God calls it an "evil heart of unbelief" and traces it to willful rebellion.

What are some other characteristics of the Grasshopper Complex?

A Distorted Self-Image

Let's reread the report of the ten fearful spies: "There also we saw the Nephilim ... and we became like grasshoppers in our own sight, and so we were in their sight" (Nm 13:33).

Note well that when the spies saw themselves as grasshoppers they immediately assumed that the Canaanites saw them as grasshoppers too! We all think that people perceive us just as we perceive ourselves.

A child who is told by his parents that he is dumb, doomed to fail, and ugly will think that that's the way everyone else sees him. A person who sees himself as a loser believes others see him that way; worse, he will most likely act like one. Our self-perception is the foundation on which we build our dreams, whether good or evil.

Looked at in one way, the spies' self-evaluation appeared humble: "We are but grasshoppers!" But in point of fact, this was nothing but a confession of their own unbelief; it was an insult to God. Why should anyone who trusts the Almighty see himself as a grasshopper?

Interestingly, the spies were wrong when they said that the Canaanites saw them as grasshoppers. In reality, the Canaanites were frightened out of their wits. Thirty-eight years later when the Israelites finally did make serious plans to enter the land, another generation of spies went to Jericho and made contact with Rahab the harlot. Working in the town brothel, she knew the sentiment of the town toward the Israelites. She reported, "I know that the Lord has given you the land, and that the terror of you has fallen on us, and that all the inhabitants of the land have melted away before you" (Jos 2:9).

Far from seeing the Israelites as grasshoppers, the Canaanites saw them as giants! They were terrified, wondering why it took the Israelites so long to claim their inheritance. Rahab understood the issues even better than the enlightened Israelites, for she went on to say that Jericho had heard of the miracles God had done, "And when we heard it, our hearts melted and no courage remained in any man any longer because of you; for the Lord your God, He is God in heaven above and on earth beneath" (Jos 2:11). She knew who God was, even if God's own people had their doubts!

If we see Satan as unbeatable, *he is.* But we can never see Satan for what he truly is until we see God for what He is—and ourselves for what we are in Christ. As Christians we must see ourselves in Christ as forgiven, accepted, ascended, and victorious. Then we will see Satan as defeated, and well within the range of our spiritual artillery. Regardless of the walls Satan hides behind, he can be routed and dethroned.

The Grasshopper Complex causes us to feel inferior to situations and even people that we, under God, are well able to confront. Like looking into a bent mirror, we distort ourselves, our enemies, our challenges, and even our God.

And there is more.

A Double Mind

Those who see themselves as grasshoppers constantly shift their focus, looking for some lodestar to follow. At times they do think about the promises of God, but such moments give way to the supposed benefits of unbelief. They keep one eye on the world and one shifting eye on God.

When the people heard the report of the ten spies, they fell into an emotional swamp. They cried all night and grumbled against Moses and Aaron, saying, "Would that we had died in the land of Egypt! Or would that we had died in this wilderness" (Nm 14:2).

The next step was to appoint a captain who would lead

them back into Egypt. And when Joshua and Caleb tried to persuade the people to drop those plans and get on with believing the Almighty for victory, the congregation responded by saying that these two optimists should be stoned. So much for the benefits of faith!

Needless to say, the people conveniently forgot that their stay in Egypt had not been entirely pleasant. They could not remember the slavery, the beatings, and the untimely deaths of their relatives and friends. Rather they spoke of the security Egypt had offered them. With one foot in the desert and one foot back in Egypt, they had no feet left to take them into the Promised Land.

James reminds us that when we ask for wisdom we should "ask in faith without any doubting, for the one who doubts is like the surf of the sea driven and tossed by the wind. For let not that man expect that he will receive anything from the Lord, being a double-minded man, unstable in all his ways" (Jas 1:6-8). Double-mindedness spills over into all of life.

The Israelites were brought out of Egypt so that they might be brought into Canaan. Now they stood poised between these two events, fearful to move ahead and yet unable to go back. With neither option a distinct possibility, they were condemned to wander in no-man's-land. They were consigned to the desert until all the adults (except Joshua and Caleb) would die.

I'm told that the Greeks had a race in which a man would stand with one foot on one horse and his other foot on a second horse. The man was able to ride in that fashion as long as the horses stayed together, but when they began to separate, he had a decision to make!

Double-mindedness is a leading cause of the Grasshopper Complex. The eye that shifts its focus between God and the world will lack the stability to take confident steps in exploring new horizons for the glory of God.

The Desire for Security

Another motivation of the Israelite multitude was *fear*, the fear that they would fail in warfare. They believed, contrary to God's promises, that they would all be killed. Anything is better than death!

The argument to stay in the desert seemed unassailable: *If they didn't fight, they couldn't lose!* The choice was between living in the familiar wilderness and risking the possibility of being beaten by an unfamiliar foe. The Canaanites would probably not leave their walled cities to harass the Israelites in a barren wilderness. Therefore, if the Israelites simply refused to accept the challenge of battle, they would not have to cope with the fear of failure.

We are often critical of Peter, who began to sink when walking on the water to go to Jesus. We chide him for taking his eyes off Christ. But we ought to commend him for at least being willing to take the risk of hopping out of the boat and trying to walk on the water. Though he wavered in the process, he took the risk of trusting Christ for a miracle. The other men were in no danger of drowning for they played it safe and stayed in the boat.

Some people avoid failing only because they never have a decent chance to fail. They play it safe, taking no risks at all.

To them security is such a high priority that they would prefer to do nothing than try something that might not succeed.

The Despising of Weakness

Perhaps the Israelites thought that they should wait until they were as strong as the Canaanites before going to war with them. But God did not want them to be strong. He was quite willing for them to remain weak so that He could make up for their deficiencies. Strategy and strength would have its place, but faith in His promises was even more important.

We often speak about "God-given strength," but we must also become acquainted with "God-given weakness." When God wanted to use Paul in a greater way, He gave him a "thorn in the flesh." When Paul prayed that it might be taken away, he was told that the grace of God would be sufficient for him. Paul replied, "Therefore I am well content with weaknesses, with insults, with distresses, with persecutions, with difficulties, for Christ's sake; *for when I am weak, then I am strong*" (2 Cor 12:10, italics mine.)

Jacob was made physically weak by God on the eve of his encounter with his estranged brother, Esau. Twenty years earlier he had wronged his brother, and now he expected hostility, perhaps even a fight. God touched the hollow of the patriarch's thigh so that he faced his brother limping (see Gn 32:22-32). Nothing could have forced him to trust in God like being made weak at the very point where he needed to be strong. By nature we seldom trust God *unless we have to.*

We must not despise weaknesses, for they are a gift from

God. In their place we must put the promises of God: the Lord loves to use these infirmities to turn our attention toward Him.

Is it any wonder that Moses later told the people that those who were afraid of battle should stay home? The priests, said Moses, should calm the people, reminding them that because the Lord was with them they were not to panic, "For the Lord your God is the one who goes with you, to fight against your enemies, to save you" (Dt 20:4). But to the fearful the officers should say, "Who is the man that is afraid and fainthearted? Let him depart and return to his house, so that he might not make his brothers' hearts melt like his heart" (Dt 20:8). Better to stay home than to spread fear among those who are preparing to trust God to win a victory. Fear is contagious!

There is a remedy for the Grasshopper Complex. It is to unite with those who have the courage to take their resources and then *add God.* Faced with a clear command from God, we can go forward and claim the territory He has allotted us.

Identifying Our Complex

We have all seen ourselves in these descriptions of the Grasshopper Complex. We have all shrunk from doing the will of God because we were overwhelmed by our insecurities and fears. We have felt that God has given us a burden too heavy to bear.

I'm told that when American troops came to one of the concentration camps in Germany some of the prisoners did not rejoice. They came out of the barracks, heard the good news, and then walked quietly back to their barren cells. They had been so used to confinement and abuse that they feared freedom!

Failure is addictive. If we have a string of failures in our past, we may cringe from the challenge of spiritual growth and victory. The Grasshopper Complex makes us content with mediocrity and spiritual sterility. Ignoring those barriers that stand between us and spiritual growth initially seems more secure, but it is highly unrewarding.

Think with me about the "territory" God may want you to inherit, and about the "walled city" standing between you and your inheritance:

- the distress of a bad marriage
- bitterness from being wronged
- the fear of establishing friendships because of past abuse
- compulsive hidden addictions that are sapping all of your emotional and spiritual energy
- fractured friendships
- failing health
- a fear of failure that causes instability

The roadblocks that exist between you and your promised land may appear formidable. In your depression you are unable to even think about the possibility of demolishing the strongholds. In short, emotional and spiritual wholeness may appear impossible.

Do not be discouraged. Someone has said that *if you are not called to the impossible you have never been called!*

"God is honored," said one man, "when we choose a task so large that if God doesn't undertake we will be taken under!" Everyone who has ever followed God has had to take some risks, humanly speaking. No one can get to the top of the mountain by following the path of least resistance.

Perhaps you are discouraged because of past disappointments. You remember when you armed yourself with the promises of God but He apparently did not come through for you. You are afraid to trust Him because you think He left you stranded in the moment of need.

That happened to the Israelites too. They did make a rather valiant effort to take the land after all, but they were as easily beaten as grasshoppers!

Let's find out why.

Chapter Two

When Faith Doesn't Work
(Read Numbers 14:39-45; Deuteronomy 1:41-46)

Is it possible to fail while relying on God? Before you say no, read on.

We left the Israelites at the door of the Promised Land, afraid to go in. They said it would be better to return to Egypt than to face the challenge of conquering Canaan. They wept as they heard Moses deliver this judgment from God: " 'As I live,' says the Lord, 'just as you have spoken in My hearing, so I will surely do to you; your corpses shall fall in this wilderness, even all your numbered men, according to your complete number from twenty years old and upward, who have grumbled against Me'" (Nm 14:28-29).

It was a long night. The people mourned greatly; the thought of not seeing the land they had dreamed about was a crushing blow. Of what value would their lives be in the bleak, hot desert? Thirty-eight years (making a total of forty) would be added to their senseless wanderings (see Dt 2:14; see also Nm 14:34). And they were doomed to die in the desert, their bones bleached in the hot sun.

Quite understandably, some of the Israelites rethought their original decision and determined to conquer the land after all. They realized how wrong they had been in seeing themselves as *grasshoppers* in the midst of *giants;* now they determined to see themselves as *giants* in the midst of *grass-hoppers*. They would show their bravery; God would be with them, just as He promised.

But it was not to be.

We read, "In the morning, however, they rose up early and went up to the ridge of the hill country, saying, 'Here we are; we have indeed sinned, but we will go up to the place which the Lord has promised'" (Nm 14:40). Despite a stern warning from Moses that they should not undertake this brave military venture, they pushed ahead with their new plans. Better late than never.

The saga continues: "But they went up heedlessly to the ridge of the hill country; neither the ark of the covenant of the Lord nor Moses left the camp" (v. 44). Though Moses and the ark stayed behind, God of course would be with them—of what value are His promises if He does not live up to them? Now at last they would be able to make up for their misdeeds.

But despite their bravery and apparent faith, we read a sad report: "Then the Amalekites and the Canaanites who lived in that hill country came down, and struck them and beat them down as far as Hormah" (v. 45). *Beaten like grasshoppers!*

Many years later Moses recounted these events, adding some vivid imagery. He said that the people acted presump-tuously, and he described what happened: "And the Amorites who lived in that hill country came out against you, and chased you as bees do, and crushed you from Seir to Hormah. Then you returned and wept before the Lord; but the Lord did not listen to your voice, nor give ear to you" (Dt 1:44-45).

I recall my father running from a swarm of bees. He couldn't travel fast or far enough! That's the way the Israelites looked when they tried to take territory for God. Where were His promises? Why did He forsake them in their hour of need? Why did He allow His people to be humiliated in the presence of pagans?

Though they had apparently reversed their self-perception and entered this battle as giants, they were as easily beaten as grasshoppers. Their original evaluation of their size seemed to be correct.

We seldom hear about the sin of presumption today. Like the Israelites, we have a tendency to rush into situations thinking we know in advance exactly what God wants us to do. We may even pray, asking Him to bless our plans. We may claim a passage of Scripture and expect God to do as we think He should. Yet in the end we are beaten, trampled by the enemy. The battle isn't even close. Where have we gone wrong?

There are several different kinds of presumption. One refers to the sin of deliberately *defying the Almighty.* No doubt we all have at some time planned to sin with the intention of confessing it later. In Numbers 15:30 we read: "But the person who does anything defiantly, whether he is native or an alien, that one is blaspheming the Lord; and that person shall be cut off from among his people." The word *defiantly* is the synonym for "a high hand," that is, someone who has raised his hand against the Almighty in open rebellion. Generally, this kind of presumption involves sinning with full knowledge.

There is a second kind of presumption: It is a *careless application of the promises and will of God.* We can easily do what seems good to us without consulting God in prayer and in His Word.

At this point I must make a distinction between promises that have to do with salvation and those that speak about

Christian living and victory. Let it be said with clarity that those who come to Christ, transferring their trust to Him, always receive the gift of eternal life (see Jn 3:36). God *immediately* answers the prayer of the person who understands that Christ's death was a sacrifice for sinners and therefore comes to humbly accept that free gift. There is but one condition to receive the promise of salvation: Faith.

Promises that have to do with Christian living are just as certain and therefore equally worthy of our trust. But though we also receive them in faith, their application may take time, prayer, and conflict. And our faith may sometimes be sorely tested when we try to experience their power.

What is more, it is possible to use these promises presumptuously, that is, without considering the interpretations and conditions that are attached to them.

That's what happened to the Israelites. They thought they had a promise in their hands, but they could not get God to honor it. Though they showed apparent bravery and courage, God disappointed them.

Why didn't this promise work?

A Wrong Interpretation

The Lord gave a promise to Moses: "Send out for yourself men so that they may spy out the land of Canaan, which I am going to give to the sons of Israel" (Nm 13:2).

Interestingly, God did not say exactly *when* He would give the land to the sons of Israel, though the implication was that it could happen as soon as the spies brought back a favorable report. But when the Israelites accepted the majority report, circumstances changed.

What a difference a day made! God had given them a new command, namely to live in the desert for thirty-eight more years. This was a new era with a new agenda. God's original promise would still be fulfilled, but at a different time, with a different generation.

Some Christians have been disappointed with God because they have taken passages which do not apply to them and yet insisted that God be held to these promises.

First, this can be done by applying a promise to a wrong time period. For example, there are passages that teach that Christ died to redeem our bodies as well as our souls (see Is 53:4-5; see also Mt 8:17). Some interpret these verses to mean that we can have physical healing whenever we want it. But this ignores the fact that the Bible also teaches that we will not see the fulfillment of these aspects of redemption until we are resurrected into glory (see 1 Cor 15:42-54). Just as Christ came to redeem us from sin, but yet we have a sinful nature, so our new bodies have been paid for but we will not enjoy them until we are transformed at the rapture.

The bottom line is, we cannot insist that God heal us whenever we are sick (though He often does so). People who claim healing in all instances, insisting that God must remain true to His promise, often feel betrayed. They think that God has been unfaithful, when actually they have interpreted Him to have promised more in this age than He has. Thus sometimes believers have presumptuously commanded God to heal or perform a miracle, just as if He had placed Himself at our beck and call.

Interestingly, John the Baptist evidently fell into the error of misreading the time when a promise would be applied. While sitting in prison, he doubtless remembered the prophecy of Isaiah that when the Messiah came, He would "proclaim liberty to captives, and freedom to prisoners" (Is 61:1). Yet now John was in prison and his cousin who claimed to be the Messiah did nothing. So John sent a delegation to Christ, asking, "Are You the Expected One, or shall we look for someone else?" (Mt 11:3).

In response, Jesus reminded John that miracles were being done, then added, "Blessed is he who keeps from stumbling over Me" (v. 6). John made the same mistake as those who think that God is always obligated to heal us. He misinterpreted the timing and application of that promise. Isaiah's prophecy will be fulfilled in its completeness only when Christ returns in glory and establishes His kingdom.

A second kind of misinterpretation is when we go beyond the promises in the Bible and put words in God's mouth. Those who fall into this error imply that God has made promises about matters that are not even found in His Word.

Some writers teach that we can get whatever we want from God. If we claim it, God will do it for us. "When you confess Jesus as the best businessman in the world, it is amazing how much money He will make for you," writes Norvel Hayes in *How to Live and Not Die* (Tulsa: Harrison House, 26). Just think of it! A God who will make us money if we have the right attitude of heart and make the right "confession"!

The author also writes, "If you believe that God won't get you out of a wheelchair or that God might not choose to heal you, your thinking is goofed up. You need to have your mind blasted" (p. 65). Jesus then becomes to us whatever we want, a businessman, a healer, a miracle worker.

It was this mentality that caused Satan to tempt Christ: "If You are the Son of God, throw Yourself down from here; for it is written, 'He will give His angels charge concerning You to guard You,' and 'On their hands they will bear You up, lest You strike Your foot against a stone'" (Lk 4:9-11). When quoting Psalm 91:11-12, Satan conveniently omitted part of the phrase: "To guard you *in all your ways.*" This was a promise for those who were being guided by God, not an invitation for anyone to force God to do a miracle by jumping from the pinnacle of the temple and then holding Him responsible if there was no dramatic rescue. Jesus answered with another Scripture: "You shall not put the Lord your God to the test" (Lk 4:12).

With reckless abandon some people begin to claim this or that, insisting that God has obligated Himself to respond. Then when it does not happen they try to find some reason (usually a lack of faith or someone else's sin) why they didn't receive the blessings promised.

My point is not that God no longer does miracles today, for we know He does. But it is presumptuous to insist that we can command Him to do whatever we think He should.

Of course committed believers will pray "without ceasing," bringing every detail before the throne of God. Sometimes God may give us the faith to trust Him for money, a better job, or healing. But because He has not promised these things, we must let Him make all final decisions. We should not think that He has obligated Himself to answer according to our desires.

Rule Number One in applying the promises of God is that *we be sure to claim a promise that is clearly intended for us* (of which there are many). Requests that go beyond what God has said may or may not be answered by the Almighty.

A Wrong Attitude

Read this passage and tell me whether the Israelites were living in complete submission to God: "In the morning, however, they rose up early and went up to the ridge of the hill country, saying, 'Here we are; we have indeed sinned, but we will go up to the place which the Lord has promised'" (Nm 14:40).

They did admit their sin; just in passing they mentioned it. But it seemed rather trivial since God had forgiven them. So they said, "We have sinned, *but*...."

Recall that when King Saul disobeyed a clear command to exterminate the Amalekites, he responded, "I have sinned; but please honor me now before the elders of my people" (1 Sm 15:30).

We've all heard confessions like that, haven't we?

"I have sinned, *but* everyone is doing it."

"I have sinned, *but* no one else knows."

"I have sinned, *but* I was tempted beyond what I could bear."

"I have sinned, *but* look at what he did to me."

I do not wish to imply that the children of Israel were not forgiven, for they were. But their rather casual remark about their sin showed that they were unwilling to accept the discipline God had prescribed for them. They thought that the consequences of their disobedience should be behind them, since they were forgiven.

They presumed that God's blessing would go with them even though they had not submitted to His authority. But as we have learned, promises that pertain to a life of victory and fruitfulness, promises that speak about entering our Canaan land, always demand submission, conflict, and persistence.

For example, we have all heard the promise "Resist the devil and he will flee from you," but often we fail to read the whole verse, "Submit therefore to God. Resist the devil and he will flee from you" (Jas 4:7). The extent of our submission to God will determine the extent of our ability to resist the devil.

The disciples were given authority over all demons (see Lk 9:1), yet in the same chapter, just a few days later, they met a demon they were unable to cast out (v. 40). Christ traced their inability to apply His promise to unbelief, but Matthew records that He also told them, "But this kind does not go out except by prayer and fasting" (Mt 17:21). Faith is always the one indispensable ingredient in applying the promises of God. However, our faith is built up through the inner disciplines of the soul such as prayer, yieldedness, and fasting. We can never take the promises of God for granted.

Rule Number Two for applying the promises of God is that *we be wholly yielded to God in every aspect of our lives.*

A Wrong Motive

What was the Israelites' motive in reversing their earlier reluctance to conquer the land? Though not expressly stated, they apparently thought that this heroic act would cause God to reverse the severe discipline He had prescribed. Perhaps they reasoned that God would say, "Well, I told them they could not enter the land, but they appear so determined that I will change My mind and help them to conquer it after all."

Think of how often we pray to God for the sole purpose of avoiding personal discomfort. This kind of praying can please God only if our desires are subject to a higher motivation, namely, the glory of God. As Christ put it, "And whatever you ask in My name, that will I do, that the Father may be glorified in the Son" (Jn 14:13).

One mark of total submission is our willingness to endure hardship (yes, that includes pain) if God is thereby glorified. Just ask Christ in Gethsemane if it is always God's will that we avoid heartache. "Not My will, but Thine be done" is the model for all of us to follow.

The Israelites should have been willing to accept God's judgment on them, no matter how disappointing and harsh. Committed believers say, "Let God be God."

How often when praying for relief from suffering do we ask ourselves what God may want to teach us in our trials? Rather, like children in a candy store, we point to any one of a number of enticing options, hoping that we will get what we want right now.

Rule Number Three in applying the promises of God is that *our motives be purified;* we must seek the glory of God alone. The eye of faith looks beyond the promise to God's purposes. In the final analysis all prayer must be subject to the will of God.

As we shall see in the following chapters, God demonstrated His faithfulness to Israel in many different ways. Not one of His promises failed, but there was a price that had to be paid. Privileges entail responsibilities.

Facing the Future

In British Columbia, five hundred miles northeast of Vancouver, the Fraser River parts into two streams—one runs east to the Atlantic Ocean, the other west to the Pacific. Once the water has parted, its direction is fixed. The fork in the river is known as the Great Divide.

The Israelites, in an act of cowardice, had made a decision that could not be reversed. They would be haunted by the realization that they had missed an incredible opportunity.

In his novel *The Fall,* French philosopher Albert Camus paints a frightening picture of a man who had to live with haunting regret because he failed to rescue a woman from suicide. Here is a summary of what happened:

That particular night in November, he was returning to the West Bank; it was past midnight, and a rainy mist was falling. On the bridge he passed a figure leaning over the railing and seeming to stare at the river. He made out the slim form of a young woman dressed in black. A moment later he heard the sound of a body striking the water. As he turned he heard a cry for help which was repeated several times, then ceased. The silence seemed interminable. He wanted to run yet did not stir. He told himself he had to be quick, but then an irresistible weakness settled over him. "Too late ... too far ..." he told himself, then slowly in the rain he went away and informed no one.

This failure of nerve on the Seine River in Paris so haunted the man that he could not get away from the river, regardless of where he traveled in the world. The flowing water awaited him everywhere. On the last page of the novel he returns to the scene of his cowardice and cries out into the night and into the river, "O, young woman, throw yourself into the water again so that I may a second time have the chance of saving *both* of us" (*The Fall* [New York: Alfred A. Knopf, 1982] 147).

Each day of our lives, it is said, in small but important ways we prepare ourselves for that moment in life where we shall die once the death of courage, or live to die a thousand times a coward.

Like it or not, the Israelites had made their choice. At Kadesh Barnea they chose the way of the coward, and now they had to live with the consequences God mapped out for them. To return to yesterday was impossible. God would not give that generation another chance. They would never be able to prove their bravery; they would not see the precious land.

Did this mean they had lost their reason to live? No, *a thousand times no.* Though their future in the land was ruined, their lives were not. For they had the opportunity to get to know God in the desert. He could become as precious to them as they desired.

God is more interested in what we *are* than in where we live or even what we accomplish; there was still a life to be lived and dreams to be fulfilled. There in the desert they would experience the provision and care of God. He would not abandon them just because they had chosen the wrong fork in the road.

The geographical restrictions imposed by God did not necessitate comparable spiritual restrictions. Even though they would never see God's power in conquering their enemies, they could love and worship the Almighty in the desert.

If they had the faith to see it, there was plenty of reason to hope.

Some who read this book may have made bad choices that are impossible to rectify. You have taken the wrong direction and there is no hope of ever getting back to the main road. You may have passed your private Kadesh Barnea. But this does not mean that you have to see yourself as a grasshopper for the rest of your life. There are oases in your desert that await discovery.

However, in a larger sense, no Christian living today is barred from the spiritual promised land. Our promised land can be enjoyed despite the wrong choices and mistakes of the past. There is a world to be explored, a relationship that needs to be nurtured. God is still waiting to show Himself strong in behalf of those who fear Him. "The Lord your God is in your midst, a victorious warrior. He will exult over you with joy, He will be quiet in His love, He will rejoice over you with shouts of joy" (Zep 3:17).

I do not know your specific need, but I can assure you that "His divine power has granted to us everything pertaining to life and godliness, through the true knowledge of Him who called us by His own glory and excellence" (2 Pt 1:3). God is as ready to help us face our wrong choices as He was to help the Israelites face theirs.

How do we tap into these resources? We link our arms with God when we accept what Peter calls "His precious and magnificent promises" (v. 4). The gap between God's side of the agreement (the promises) and our side (our performance) must be bridged. When God is tested, He is found faithful.

What promises do belong to us? How much should we trust

God for? How do we apply the promises so that we can get out of our rut, that prison of the soul that casts a pall on everything we do? How do we overcome the Grasshopper Complex?

We will address these questions in the following chapters.

Chapter Three

Listening to the Right Voice
(Read Joshua 1)

In an army the single most important lesson you learn is to listen to and obey the commander. Presumably he knows more than you do and has a strategy that works. It's not important for you to understand the whys and wherefores; the key is to obey his explicit commands.

Therefore, the communications system is crucial the moment a war begins. Proper two-way communication inspires courage, gives guidance, and unifies the attack. If the troops are cut off from contact with headquarters they become isolated and confused.

So the enemy either tries to intercept the messages or else feeds some wrong signals to the troops. The result is that they either hear nothing or are misled.

There are many Christians today who are trying to fight battles with their communications equipment in disrepair. They are not in daily contact with God and therefore suffer from discouragement and spiritual fatigue. They are, in effect, fighting on their own without direction and confidence.

Or, worse, these believers are following the advice of an enemy; they are hearing the wrong signals. They are listening to what the Canaanites are whispering behind walls rather than hearing the shouts of God from heaven.

God knew that if Joshua and his troops were to conquer a series of pagan fortifications they would have to keep in constant contact with headquarters. Never should they plan an attack without checking with the Commander in Chief.

Joshua's job description was rather clear: "Moses My servant is dead; now therefore arise, cross this Jordan, you and all this people, to the land which I am giving to them, to the sons of Israel" (Jos 1:2). Moses had been forbidden to lead the nation into the Promised Land, and now he was dead. His understudy was given this formidable responsibility.

Joshua had to motivate the people to action. The nation had lived in relative peace for forty years. There were no serious enemies in the desert. But now that would have to change—*war was inevitable.*

But war was not all he had to prepare them for. Recall that the people did not have to work hard in the desert. They had not planted a crop nor watered a single garden. They did not have to pull weeds or build walls. God had provided all their needs by sending manna every morning. They had become accustomed to a comfortable lifestyle.

Paul said that he had learned contentment in any state he experienced (see Phil 4:11). That is certainly an admirable goal, but there is also a destructive kind of contentment. We can become content with mediocrity, content with failure, and yes, content with sin. The Israelites had become content to take the easy path.

They needed an incredible injection of courage. They craved assurance that they were not in this alone and that there were benefits to taking a God-ordained risk. The Almighty had said He would take up their cause and fight for them, but how could they be sure? They were afraid.

There is nothing wrong with fear, as long as it is aimed in the right direction. What we fear determines whether we will move forward or retreat in our spiritual lives. John Wesley said, "Give me a hundred men who fear nothing but sin, and desire nothing but God, and I will shake the world.... Such alone will overthrow the kingdom of Satan and build up the kingdom of God on earth."

Unfortunately, our fear is often misdirected. We fear change; we fear confrontation; we fear our past; we fear the future; we fear poverty; we fear war; we fear death.

Think of how differently we would live if we feared God, feared compromise with sin, and feared unbelief! When David listed some of the characteristics of the one who feared the Lord, he added, "He will not fear evil tidings; His heart is steadfast, trusting in the Lord" (Ps 112:7). The choice is clear: Either we will fear God or we will fear our enemies. To put it differently, *if we fear God we need fear nothing else.*

What would shake the nation out of its sleep and awaken it to the possibility of a victory? Where would the assurances of courage and guidance come from? How was Joshua to dissipate misdirected fear?

The key to it all is found in God's command to Joshua: "Only be strong and very courageous; be careful to do according to all the law which Moses My servant commanded you; do not turn from it to the right or to the left, so that you may have success wherever you go" (Jos 1:7).

Joshua would have to be wholly absorbed in studying and applying the Law of God. He would have to follow God, avoiding distractions on his right and on his left. God now gives more details: "This book of the Law shall not depart from your mouth, but you shall meditate on it day and night, so that you may be careful to do according to all that is written in it; for then you will make your way prosperous, and then you will have success" (v. 8). For Joshua the Word of God comprised the five books called the Pentateuch. These books, written by Moses, would be all he needed to guide him in his battles.

What was Joshua to do with the Word of God? First, He was to *speak* it. The physical act of speaking God's Word back to Him would inspire faith and embed the commands and promises in his memory.

Second, he was to *meditate* on it day and night. The reason was simple: meditation was the means by which his mind would be made pure, free from distractions and misdirected fear. It would give him further understanding of God's will and provide the instruction and faith needed to take some reasonable risks in capturing the giants of Jericho.

Then he was to *do* what the Lord commanded. Obedience would result in blessing. He would prosper and become successful in his tactical maneuvers as he captured the land for God.

Speaking God's Word and meditating upon it enables us to put it into practice. Recently I spoke to a man who works for an employer who berates him at every opportunity. Every morning this committed Christian has to listen to false accusations and criticism. How does he maintain his cool in such a hostile environment? He says what keeps him on track spiritually is that he spends two hours every morning in Bible memorization and prayer. This gives him the spiritual stamina to take verbal abuse with a Christlike spirit.

George Müeller (1805–98) is famous for establishing orphanages in England and depending on God alone for the finances to run them. In 1841 he made a life-changing discovery. He writes, "I saw more clearly than ever, that the first great and primary business to which I ought to attend every day was, to have my soul happy in the Lord." He goes on to explain that serving the Lord and even finding how he might glorify Him is secondary. Before breakfast he would meditate on the Scriptures until his soul was "nourished." Little wonder Müeller so consistently received his marching orders from God.

Joshua knew that the voice he listened to would determine the direction he would walk. If he listened to his emotions he would remain content in the desert. If he could hear the whispers of the Canaanites he would be intimidated. If he heard the criticism of his troops he would be distracted. Only if he regularly heard the voice of God would he have the courage to do what seemed impossible.

God's Commands to Joshua

Let's consider three commands God gave Joshua.

1. Get Up: Face the Enemy
"Arise, cross this Jordan, you and all this people, to the land which I am giving to them, to the sons of Israel" (Jos 1:2).

This nation which had grown so complacent in the desert would now have to confront the enemy. By crossing the Jordan River, they would be throwing down the gauntlet; this was a declaration of war. Their new camp on the west bank of the river would be a base for launching attacks on the enemy. But it would also be an invitation for the enemy to attack *them.*

The decision to cross the river was like jumping into the ring with a boxer who has been impatiently waiting to pin you to the floor. Once you have crossed the ropes the battle is inevitable.

Similarly, we must make a decision to confront the challenges that stand between us and spiritual progress. We cannot avoid the enemy and expect him to go away. We must take the risk of confrontation.

2. Walk: Fight the Enemy

"Every place on which the sole of your foot treads, I have given it to you, just as I spoke to Moses" (Jos 1:3).

Just to make sure that Joshua understood that the title deed was his, God put the promise in the past tense. "I *have* given it to you, just as I spoke to Moses."

A little boy came to the Washington Monument and noticed a guard standing by it.

"I want to buy it."

"How much do you have?" asked the guard.

"Thirty-five cents."

"You need to understand three things," the guard explained. "First, thirty-five cents is not enough to purchase the monument, in fact, thirty-five million dollars is not enough. Second, the Washington Monument is not for sale; and third, if you are an American citizen, you already own it!"

How often we ask God for blessings that are already ours in Christ! Paul wrote, "Blessed be the God and Father of our Lord Jesus Christ, who has blessed us with every spiritual blessing in the heavenly places in Christ" (Eph 1:3). The blessing and the victory are already ours.

But there is a catch: The blessings that are legally ours cannot be experienced apart from conflict, vigilance, and much faith. The legal privileges are given to all believers; the experience of them is limited to those who strive against all odds.

Recently I spoke with a family that had experienced specific demonic attacks because of the unholy influence of parents who were into the occult. The harassment was persistent and powerful. And though they as Christians have authority over the enemy, he did not let go without a fight.

When the Lord told Joshua to walk, it was not a "cake walk." In fact, this walk would attract focused hostility. The promise in his hand had to be claimed by his feet. The Canaanites were not about to roll over and play dead.

It is absolutely crucial that we remember there is a vast difference between our legal rights and the experience of them. Knowing a promise is quite different from claiming it.

Here is a short preview of the struggles that accepting the title deed to the land would entail for the Israelites:

(1) Conflict. There were several powerful warring tribes to be fought. Regardless of how many differences they had among themselves, they would unite against Israel. City after city would have to be conquered individually. And there would be some casualties among Joshua's troops.

(2) Time. The conquests in the Book of Joshua span about fourteen years. It was not a matter of walking into the land and taking possession in an afternoon. We would like to think that our victory can be claimed in one act of surrender and faith. But the battles are continuous and each takes time.

(3) Unity. No single Israelite could win this war alone. In fact, all twelve tribes had to fight together.

Many years earlier, Reuben, Gad, and one-half of the tribe of Manasseh had made an agreement with Moses that would allow them to settle on the eastern side of the Jordan River. Moses agreed to their request as long as they promised to help their brothers and sisters rout the Canaanites. Joshua now honored their request and discussed the details with them (see Jos 1:12-18).

All the tribes were needed to fight. If Joshua had given his permission to let these tribes go their way without participating in the conflict, Israel would have been much weaker and the conquest of the land would have taken longer.

One of the greatest failures of the American church is individualism. We are determined to live the Christian life alone and on our own terms. We think that because our relationship with God is personal, all our battles must be personal too.

Just as all twelve tribes would participate in defeat as well as victory, so the whole body of Christ is involved in our struggles. No man lives to himself; no man dies to himself. Every one of us contributes to the strength or weakness of the believing church.

(4) Knowledge. Joshua sent the spies into the land to help him understand the enemy and locate their points of weakness. Taking the land involved strategy and planning. Each battle was different, and Joshua had to be alert enough to know the leading of God.

3. Stand: Crush the Enemy

"No man will be able to stand before you all the days of your life. Just as I have been with Moses, I will be with you; I will not fail you or forsake you" (Jos 1:5).

God specified the boundaries of the land that rightfully belonged to the Israelites. This was to be the territory they would trust God to help them conquer.

What strikes us is the utter impossibility of compromise with the Canaanites. Joshua understood that he could not show any mercy to these pagans. Either they would have the land or he would; the only hope for rest was to totally subdue them.

This gives us a clue as to why it is so difficult for us to live a fruitful Christian life. We have enemies who seek our utter destruction. The world, the flesh, and the devil all are nipping at our heels to keep us discouraged and turn us away from Christ. When these enemies are given entry they become strong and seek total control; when they are subdued they seek a temporary truce.

All compromise with sin weakens us. Our conflict with sin and Satan must always be a fight to the finish.

God's Commands to Us

God has staked out an inheritance for us just as He did for Israel. Paul wrote, "He predestined us to adoption as sons through Jesus Christ to Himself, according to the kind intention of His will" (Eph 1:5). Indeed the word *predestine* was used of surveyors who would map out territory before the people arrived. God predestined us to be the sons of God and elevated us to be "heirs of God, and joint-heirs with Christ" (Rom 8:17, KJV).

God has given many promises describing what it means to walk in the blessings of our inheritance. Like Joshua we must listen to God's voice, not that of our emotions or the misleading information that comes from the circumstances of life.

Imagine going into battle with a two-way radio, receiving constant guidance and assurances from a commander who has all knowledge and all power at his disposal. Despite the setbacks and pain we could continue with renewed hope.

God's primary means of communication with us is through His Word. Every other voice must be tested by this clear revelation. All other guidance is subjective and therefore liable to misinterpretation and error. But the Bible is a clear and unwavering message from God to us. To paraphrase Martin Luther, "Here we stand, we can do no other."

If you are serious about wanting God to bring lasting change in your own life, identify the enemies you need to see defeated. Name three attitudes, habits, or sins that need to come under your authority. Then memorize passages of Scripture that relate to the specific areas of attack.

For example:

Anxiety. "Peace I leave with you; My peace I give to you; not as the world gives, do I give to you. Let not your heart be troubled, nor let it be fearful" (Jn 14:27).

Guilt: "If we confess our sins, He is faithful and righteous to forgive us our sins and to cleanse us from all unrighteousness" (1 Jn 1:9).

Lust: "And do not be conformed to this world, but be transformed by the renewing of your mind, that you may prove what the will of God is, that which is good and acceptable and perfect" (Rom 12:2).

Fear: "Do not fear, for I am with you; do not anxiously look about you, for I am your God. I will strengthen you, surely I will help you, surely I will uphold you with My righteous right hand" (Is 41:10).

Scripture memory is only a part of a life of meditation in the Word of God. It is absolutely essential that you and I read the Word of God each day, *seeking spiritual food and refusing to put the Bible down until our souls have been fed.* Just as our bodies cannot work without food, so our souls cannot be nourished without the Word of God. As George Müeller said, our first duty is to obtain food for the inner man. Without that, there can be no permanent change, no lasting victory over our enemies.

Satan is a thief who wants to steal all these blessings from us. He wants to occupy our mind, keep us off balance, and make us fall into confusion.

We can identify with Martin Luther, who prayed, "Dear Lord, although I am sure of my position, I cannot sustain it without Thee. Help Thou me, or I am lost."

Are there any special barriers that exist between us and spiritual progress? What are we doing to see that they are removed so that we can get on with spiritual growth?

We must come to the point in our spiritual fellowship with God that we cannot live without Him. Or better, let us hope that our times with Him are so special that *He* will miss *us* when we neglect our daily appointment in His presence!

Only if the Book of the Law did not depart out of his mouth could Joshua begin the long struggle of taking the land that God said was his.

Conflict would precede the conquest.

Doubt sees the obstacles
Faith sees the Way
Doubt sees the darksome night
Faith sees the day
Doubt dreads to take the step
Faith soars on high
Doubt whispers, "Who believes?"
Faith answers, "I."

The longer we look at God the smaller our obstacles become. The longer we look at the obstacles the smaller God becomes. The question is whether we want a big God or a big enemy. It's just a matter of perspective.

How strong is the enemy? And what is his attitude toward us? These are questions that Joshua needed answered, and we do too.

Chapter Four

A Winning Strategy
(Read Joshua 2)

How can we hope to win spiritual battles in a culture that is increasingly drifting toward pagan values?

Ours is not the first pagan society. Sometimes we think that the moral state of the world has never been worse, but it *has* been worse—some cultures have been thoroughly paganized.

Consider the land of Canaan in the time of Joshua, 1400 B.C. Here was a culture beyond redemption, beyond hope. Archeology has shown that the Canaanites participated in child sacrifice, homosexuality, idolatry, and witchcraft. And no one was taking a stand against this depraved culture. God asked that the Canaanites be exterminated, for there was literally no one left who was righteous.

Joshua was commanded to conquer the land. Every place where the Israelites would walk eventually became theirs. But the walk was not a leisurely stroll. They had to fight for every square inch.

As already mentioned, this is a striking example of the blend between God's promises and human responsibility. Yes, God said that the land was theirs, but they would have to carefully plan a strategy to crush the enemy. Their faith was not to be blind; they were to send spies and find out all that they could about Jericho. They were to investigate the resources and mental disposition of the Canaanites.

So Joshua sent some spies to gather intelligence for the coming assault on Jericho. He needed to evaluate Jericho's will to fight, and how prepared it was for a siege. His command was terse, "Go, view the land, especially Jericho" (Jos 2:1). Yes, God was with him, but Joshua still needed to know his enemy.

Today our enemy is Satan. And as the Israelites spied out Jericho, we must spy on Satan, so that "we are not ignorant of his schemes" (2 Cor 2:11).

Joshua sent only two spies into the fortified city. Thirty-eight years earlier Moses had sent twelve spies into the land. Ten returned saying that the enemy was too big for them to tackle. Only two said, "With God's help, we can!" Recall that the report of the ten demoralized the people. They revolted in fear and even planned to return to Egypt. Joshua remembered that incident all too clearly, so he sent only two—the number that had previously returned with an optimistic report. And he sent them secretly, so that they would report back to him alone. He minimized the possibility of sending a wrong message to the multitude again. The two would give him all the information he needed to mobilize the troops.

It should not surprise us that when the men looked for a place to spend the night in Jericho, they were directed to an inn run by a prostitute. Prostitution was quite common in that pagan culture. There is no evidence that the men took advantage of Rahab's sexual services. This just happened to be the best place in town to get something to eat and to find out what the citizens thought of the Israelites.

What does surprise us is that God had already begun to work in the heart of Rahab. Though she had accepted the values of her culture she would soon rise above it. This lady had an extraordinary future that she knew nothing about.

God would use Rahab in overcoming the fear that paralyzed Israel thirty-eight years earlier. From this one woman the spies would receive all the information they needed to report back to their commander.

What information did the spies gather on this fact-finding mission?

The Enemy Is Ready for Warfare

As the men walked through the gates of the city, they were instantly identified as strangers. No one knew for sure who they were, but they looked suspicious. When word reached the king of the city, he immediately assumed that these were the Israelites they had been expecting for so long. So he sent his soldiers and asked Rahab where the men were. "Bring out the men who have come to you, who have entered your house, for they have come to search out all the land" (Jos 2:3).

Though the king was terrified of Israel, he was not about to work out a peace settlement. Though he must have realized that his eventual doom was inevitable, he was prepared to fight to the death. When the people of God appeared for conflict, the enemy became angry and defensive.

Rahab took two great risks.

First, she hid the men. She showed them how they could hide among the stalks of flax she had laid on the roof (see v. 6).

That in itself was dangerous business! If she had been found out she would have been killed on the spot. Ancient cultures did not give people the benefit of a trial with legal representation. If you were deemed guilty it was all over for you.

Second, she lied, saying that the men had come, but she didn't know who they were, and at dark they had left. In fact, she suggested that the soldiers try to pursue them.

The question has often been asked: Did she do right in telling a lie? After all, she did save the lives of two of God's servants. Think of the good that came about as a result of it! What is more, telling a lie was simply accepted as part of pagan culture.

But the end does not justify the means. Whenever we lie that good might come, we actually call God's power and authority into question. Would the Almighty have been trapped if she had told the truth? Would He have said, "What will I do now? Rahab actually told the truth!"

No, if God had wanted to spare the lives of these men, He could have done so even if the truth had been told. Perhaps the men could have escaped before the soldiers got there, or maybe the soldiers themselves would have had a change of heart and let the men go free. God is never in a quandary when we tell the truth.

Lie or no lie, Rahab did identify with the men of Israel. The soldiers took her word at face value and went on a wild goose chase in the direction of the Jordan River. Needless to say, they didn't find the spies.

Let us commend Rahab for standing against the pagan culture of her day and choosing to help those whom she believed were sent by God. For all her sins, she was a woman of faith.

The spies discovered that though the enemy may live in considerable calm, the moment preparations are made for a battle latent antagonism is ignited. No doubt they reported to Joshua the fact that the Canaanites were jittery, preparing to kill the Israelites.

Frequently as a pastor I have spoken on the topic of Satan and have found that some people become so agitated that they are tempted to get up and leave (some do). Others find it difficult to read a book on how to combat Satan and his forces. They are overcome by fears that if they begin to fight they will be under vicious attack.

The two spies understood that even enemies who know they will be defeated do all the damage they can to intimidate their opponents. When God's people plan an attack, the enemy attempts a focused, angry response.

The Enemy Is Afraid

Rahab was used by God to give the spies all the information they needed. If anyone knew what the people of her day thought about the Israelites, it was she.

The information was startling but exactly what the spies had hoped to hear. Two points were of particular interest.

1. The Canaanites Knew the Rightful Owners of the Land

"I know that the Lord has given you the land, and that the terror of you has fallen on us, and that all the inhabitants of the land have melted away before you" (Jos 2:9).

The Canaanites knew they were living on land that was not

theirs. The fact that they had occupied it for centuries made little difference because it was God who made the decisions as to what belonged to whom. They were squatters, fearing eviction.

The analogy is clear. Satan knows what God has given to His people. He knows that we have been blessed with every spiritual blessing in heavenly places: a clear conscience, freedom from the power of sin, the peace of God—all these and more belong to the members of God's family. Satan fears we shall take what already belongs to us!

What caused Jericho's fear? A rumor had reached the people of how God had led the Israelites across the Red Sea. "For we have heard how the Lord dried up the water of the Red Sea before you when you came out of Egypt" (v. 10).

The Israelites were redeemed from Egypt because of the blood of a lamb that was sprinkled on their doorposts. This shielded them from the last plague in which the firstborn of every Egyptian household died. In desperation Pharaoh allowed the people to leave his country, and the Israelites experienced the miracle of the Red Sea. Egypt with its slavery was left behind, and a new adventure was about to begin by entering the Promised Land. Thus crossing the Red Sea represents salvation.

Knowledge of this worried the people of Jericho. They looked to the past and knew that there was no way they could win a war against a God who was able to redeem a whole nation.

Satan looks back to Calvary; he sees the cross of two thousand years ago and melts in terror, for he knows that his defeat is absolutely certain. He is painfully aware that those who have trusted Christ have the edge on him. Whatever the outcome of the conflicts in this world, the redeemed shall live in bliss while he (the devil and his angels) shall live in perpetual torment.

2. The Canaanites Knew of God's Power

The victory of the Red Sea, the story of God's redemption of His people, struck terror in the minds of the enemy. But they had also heard of some of the victories the Israelites had won over other kingdoms, namely the two kings of the Amorites, Sihon and Og (see Jos 2:10).

As might be expected, the Canaanites resisted Israel's rightful ownership. They were not about to surrender, though they knew they were essentially squatters. They would try to do what Satan still tries to do today: Fight a war that is impossible to win.

For every victory Satan wins, his loss is only that much greater. Let us suppose that he breaks up a marriage, holds others bound by addictions—all of these victories only add up to more eternal judgment. He will be judged for every single evil deed, and therefore each such act only adds to his final misery. He is highly intelligent but not wise. Even if he had only his best interests at heart, he would immediately cease and desist all activity against the Almighty. But he will not stop, for evil beings push compulsively ahead, regardless of their own eventual torment.

Satan does not want us to know that he is afraid. He is intelligent enough to realize that even his victories are actually defeats. He becomes impotent when approached with faith and the calm assurance that he is doomed.

"And when we heard it," Rahab continued, "our hearts

melted and no courage remained in any man any longer because of you; for the Lord your God, He is God in heaven above and on earth beneath" (v. 11). She acknowledged the weakness of these pagans in the presence of the true God.

Think of the courage that must have come to Joshua and his leaders when the spies reported that the enemy was afraid.

He did not as yet know exactly how God was going to destroy Jericho. For now it was enough for him to learn that the occupants of the city were demoralized. The God who had filled them with fear would eventually bring the city to ruin as witness to His power and justice.

Even thirty-eight years earlier, Joshua knew that the height of Jericho's walls made no difference, for one good reason: God had removed Jericho's *protection* (see Nm 14:9). The strength of the occupants of Jericho was of no account once God decided it was time for the walls to fall.

As our enemy today, Satan likewise tries to hide behind "walls." He would prefer that we think we are fighting a physical, emotional, or psychological battle rather than a spiritual one. Obviously these factors are involved in our struggles, but often they are cover for demonic activity. Thankfully, as we seek God we will discover that Satan's protection, like Jericho's, has been removed. God can demolish the walls and expose the true source of our defeats.

Joshua would soon see the enemy exposed and humiliated in his presence. As the walls would crumble, there would be no place to hide. The cover would be blown.

The Enemy Is Defeated

If there was any doubt that God was the victor in this city, Joshua had simply to consider the remarkable life of Rahab herself. She was living proof that the God of Israel could not only win a military victory but could win the heart of an individual as well.

Rahab asked the spies to make a covenant with her. Since she was kind to them, she got them to agree that she and her family would be spared from death when the Israelites came to conquer the city. The spies accepted her terms: "Our life for yours if you do not tell this business of ours; and it shall come about when the Lord gives us the land that we will deal kindly and faithfully with you" (Jos 2:14).

One final detail: She agreed to tie a scarlet rope out of the window of her house so that the Israelites would know which house to spare. All those within the house would live; all others would be killed.

With a bucket and rope she let the men down the side of the wall and told them to run west (the opposite direction from the Jordan) and stay there for three days. Later, when the king's pursuers returned, the Israelite spies left their hideout and wound their way back to Joshua. When the city was captured, the promise to Rahab was kept (see Jos 6:22-25).

Rahab was indeed a remarkable woman. She should have been killed when the Israelites finally conquered Jericho, but she did not perish with the wicked.

There are many reasons why she should have been destroyed.

First, she was condemned morally. In the Old Testament

God asked that the people stone those who participated in immorality.

Second, she was condemned religiously—she was not a Jew, and therefore was not within the stream of God's special covenants and blessing.

Third, God had told the Israelites that they should not make covenants with the people of the land, yet they made this covenant, apparently with His blessing.

Fourth, God had said that the Israelites should not marry the people of the land, and yet Rahab married an Israelite.

Think of what an exception she was to the laws God had given His people!

Why this beautiful exception?

1. Rahab Knew More Than She Realized

It was not by accident that Rahab hung a scarlet cord in the window. She did not realize it, but that cord symbolized the scarlet thread that runs throughout the whole Bible; it is a scarlet trail of blood.

That thread begins in the Garden of Eden where Adam and Eve were given animal skins to cover themselves. Already God was teaching them that there would be a cover for shame and guilt.

The scarlet thread is clearly seen in the Book of Exodus where the Israelites took the blood of a lamb and sprinkled it on the doorposts of each house to be spared the death of the firstborn.

We see that cord in the sacrifices of Leviticus, and trace it to the banks of the Jordan River where John the Baptist cried, "Behold, the Lamb of God who takes away the sin of the world!" (Jn 1:29).

Finally, we see it in the Book of Revelation where the choirs of heaven sing, "Worthy art Thou to take the book, and to break its seals; for Thou wast slain, and didst purchase for God with Thy blood men from every tribe and tongue and people and nation" (Rv 5:9).

About fourteen centuries after the time of Rahab, Jesus Christ would die on the cross and shed His blood for sinners. Included in that death would be a sacrifice for Rahab's sin.

2. She Believed What She Knew

Think of it—Rahab did not have a Bible; she lived centuries before the prophets spoke and fourteen hundred years before John 3:16 was written. She had never seen a gospel tract; no one had ever prayed for her.

Her faith was imperfect, for as we already noted, she lied. But in spite of that, she did believe. She did not hang on to her pagan religion and say, "I'm staying with the people of my culture no matter what."

What did God do for this woman? Her life was spared.

Her dignity was also spared.

What dignity can a former prostitute have? Rahab married an Israelite named Salmon (tradition says he was one of the spies), and remarkably she appears in the genealogy of Christ (see Mt 1:5). Not merely was she a prostitute but a *Gentile* prostitute! And yet—and yet, an ancestress of Christ!

Most important, Rahab's soul was saved. She believed what she knew, and it was credited to her for righteousness.

When the writer of Hebrews wanted to catalog the heroes of faith who proved their courage in overcoming the enemy, he included Rahab along with all of the "stars"—Enoch, Abraham, Moses, and David, to name a few. "By faith Rahab the harlot did not perish along with those who were disobedient, after she had welcomed the spies in peace" (Heb 11:31).

Rahab indeed is worthy of honor, for she believed in God at great personal cost. When she hid the spies she immediately became the enemy of the king of Jericho. She crossed the line with all of the risks that entailed.

Here is a woman who helped the Israelites see how distorted their Grasshopper Complex really was. The congregation back at Kadesh Barnea had totally overestimated the strength and determination of the enemy. Having perceived themselves as grasshoppers, they thought that the Canaanites perceived them the same way. But as Rahab observed, the reverse was true: The Canaanites thought *they* were grasshoppers in the sight of the "giant" Israelites!

In the early part of the last century an artist painted a picture of a chess game. The players were a young man and Satan. The young man manipulated the white pieces, Satan the black ones. If the young man were to win, he would be forever free from the power of evil; if Satan were to win, the young man would be his servant forever.

The artist, who was a great chess player, had the pieces lined up in such a way that the devil had just moved his queen and announced checkmate in four moves. The young man was seen hovering over his rook, his face pale with fear.

For years the picture hung in an art gallery with chess players from all over the world coming to ponder the configuration of the pieces, convinced that the devil had won. Yet one day a famous chess player named Paul Morphy was brought into the gallery to view the picture. He stood there, gesturing with his hands, as in his imagination he eliminated one move after another. To the amazement of all, the old man figured out a combination of moves that would defeat the devil.

"Young man, make that move!" he shouted.

Just when you and I think that the devil has outplayed us, God reminds us that there is a move we can make. The king of our Jericho may shout, "Checkmate!" But God can show us a move we can make *that has not crossed the enemy's mind.*

God has an infinite number of possibilities at His disposal. We may be boxed in, but He is not. The Israelites soon learned that God is willing to use supernatural resources to fulfill the promises He has made to His people. Even standing on the wrong side of a fast-flowing river is no obstacle to the Almighty.

There is always a move God can make.

"When He had disarmed the rulers and authorities, He made a public display of them, having triumphed over them through Him" (Col 2:15).

Chapter Five

Taking the First Step
(Read Joshua 3)

Have you identified the obstacle that exists between you and the fulfillment of God's will? Why are you unwilling to reach beyond yourself to a challenge that God has given you?

For the Israelites that obstacle was the Jordan River, which flowed between them and the Promised Land. They could not even begin to fight the enemy until they had crossed this major hurdle.

The stakes were high. There was no turning back. Behind them was the vast wasteland of the wilderness, the unending sand and barren mountains. They had endured forty painful years of God's discipline, and now it was time to move on.

If they took up the challenge, this generation of Israelites would enjoy the benefits of the land. There were gardens with cucumbers and melons, crops of grain and corn. This would be a welcome relief from the steady diet of manna they had become accustomed to in the hot desert. Now they would get water from wells and fish from the Sea of Galilee.

Bethlehem, the town where Christ would be born hundreds of years later, was on the other side of the river. Though it was now under the control of a pagan tribe, it would witness the fulfillment of the dream of the nation and the hope of the world.

Jerusalem was also on the other side of the river. This was the city that would become the spiritual and political capital of the nation; it would be the city of the temple and the priests. Outside its walls Jesus Christ, the Messiah, would eventually die as a sacrifice for sinners.

These places—and many others of future importance—were all in enemy territory. The Canaanites would have to be killed, the cities and towns liberated. But before they could conquer the land there was an impossible river to be crossed. It was a barrier that could not be wished away. The snows from Mount Hermon would cause the Jordan to swell to one hundred or even two hundred feet wide during this flood stage (see Jos 3:15).

It has been said that a journey of a thousand miles begins with a single step. And that first step is usually the most fearful—especially if it means stepping into a deep river whose swift current could sweep you away in an instant.

"The difficult we do immediately; the impossible takes a little longer," reads a sign in a business establishment. If crossing the Jordan had been merely difficult, Joshua might have predicted what God would do. But because it was *impossible*, evidently not even he knew how this would be accomplished.

Chuck Swindoll writes, "We are all faced with a series of great opportunities brilliantly disguised as impossible situations." If this was an opportunity, it certainly was well-disguised. Even the most optimistic person could not guess how this nation could be expected to get to the other side. Joshua didn't have to understand; he just had to obey.

If Egypt represents the world, and the long excursion in the desert represents the discipline every one of us experiences, then the Jordan River represents the full surrender that must precede the lifelong task of knowing God. Each of us comes to our own Jordan at some point in our lives.

What did Joshua ask the Israelites to do just before this act of conscious surrender to the will of God? And by implication what must we do if we are to make a decisive, irrevocable decision to yield to God?

Prepare Your Heart

"Then Joshua rose early in the morning; and he and all the sons of Israel set out from Shittim and came to the Jordan, and they lodged there before they crossed" (Jos 3:1). There at the edge of the Jordan River they set up camp, and spent three days preparing for a miracle. The officers gave the people instructions on the procedures for crossing the river.

Notice the spiritual preparations needed for this step of faith: "Consecrate yourselves, for tomorrow the Lord will do wonders among you" (v. 5). If the Israelites expected the Lord to fight for them, sin would have to be put away. Greed, sexual misconduct, and pride would have to be confessed and forsaken. But perhaps the greatest sin lurking in their hearts was fear, the feeling that Joshua may have misread God's instructions, or that God would allow them to go through more grief than they were prepared to handle.

Consecration also involves receiving God's promises. That is, accepting what God has said at face value. Joshua reminded the people that God would dispossess the seven pagan tribes who now occupied the land. "By this you shall know that the living God is among you, and that He will assuredly dispossess from before you the Canaanite, the Hittite, the Hivite, the Perizzite, the Girgashite, the Amorite, and the Jebusite" (v. 10). The living God would prove that He was among them, but they needed to be ready.

This does not mean that we have to be perfect before we attempt anything for God. It does mean that we must expose everything God shows us about ourselves—we must give it all to Him in honest submission. Bit by bit the change will take place.

This process of consecration, this transforming of our character, can be compared to an iceberg which has only 10 percent of its total mass above the water. As the sun shines on it, the exposed parts melt, moving the lower parts upward. As the light of God's Word works in our hearts and we change in those matters brought to our attention, we become aware of even more work that needs to be done.

So you want to take that first big step and shed the Grasshopper Complex? Put all your sin away through repentance and submission to God and His promises. Let Him change you so that you will have the strength to take God at His Word and move on to the task before you.

Our Jordan will look much smaller once we have confessed our sin and yielded wholly to God. It is not always important that we understand how God will take care of a special need. What is necessary is that we be spiritually prepared to accept whatever God might do.

Focus Your Eyes

Specific instructions were given to the people: They were to follow the ark, which would be carried by the priests through the riverbed. The masses were to maintain a distance of two thousand cubits (about a half mile) from the ark so that as many as possible could see it.

The ark was a box about 4.5 feet long, and 2.5 feet high, and 2.5 feet wide. In it was some manna, Aaron's rod, and a copy of the Ten Commandments. It had a gold top called the mercy seat, over which two statues of the cherubim stood (see Ex 25:18-19). In the tabernacle and later in the temple the ark represented the presence of God.

As Israel followed the ark, they were being led by God. To focus on God is always necessary, but now especially so, for the nation was embarking on a new adventure involving great danger. The instructions to the people were, "Do not come near it, that you may know the way by which you shall go, *for you have not passed this way before*" (Jos 3:4, italics mine).

No Israelite was expected to forge his own path. They were to go only where God Himself was leading them. They were not to be lone pioneers but were to follow their God, who would build the highway for them.

Today Christ is our ark; He is Immanuel, "God with us." He is the Good Shepherd, who leads His sheep. Sheep are not expected to find their own way; they are simply to follow the shepherd.

I've often said to missionaries on their way to a foreign country, facing all of the barriers of a new culture, language, and climate, that God is the best travel agent. He never sends

His people anywhere but that He arrives there ahead of them to prepare the way!

The author of Hebrews wrote that we should run the race of life, "fixing our eyes on Jesus, the author and perfecter of faith, who for the joy set before Him endured the cross, despising the shame, and has sat down at the right hand of the throne of God" (Heb 12:2). Jesus passed through the iron gate of death, giving us the assurance that even in that final moment we are still following our leader.

Christ would never expect us to cross a river that He Himself has not first crossed. *Everything He asks us to do is based on what He has already done; it is following a path that already has His footprints.*

Does He want us to become intimately acquainted with the Father? Look at His prayer life. Does He want us to do what is right despite the ridicule of our peers? Think of the insults He endured. Does He want us to be willing to endure emotional torture? Think of Gethsemane. Does He want us to face death with the confidence of being welcomed on the other side? Think of the cross.

In the movie *The Hiding Place* Corrie ten Boom and her sister are in a prison camp discussing their fate with other inmates. Understandably, there is a great deal of bitterness directed toward God. How could He look down from heaven and see this suffering and not intervene? But Corrie remarks, "There is no pit that is so deep, but that God is deeper still."

There is no river that God expects you to cross but that God has already crossed it. We begin with Christ on the journey, and He stays a step ahead of us to the end. Our greatest challenge is to keep our focus on Him.

Walk With Your Feet

The priests had to take a step of faith; they would have to stand in the flowing river. Joshua told them, "When you come to the edge of the waters of the Jordan, you shall stand still in the Jordan" (Jos 3:8). The water would not stop flowing until they got wet. God would do the rest.

So it was. When the priests who carried the ark stepped into the swift-flowing Jordan, God intervened. "The waters which were flowing down from above stood and rose up in one heap, a great distance away at Adam.... So the people crossed opposite Jericho" (v. 16).

As near as archeologists can determine, the city of Adam, where the waters were cut off, is about fifteen miles north of the Dead Sea. This provided a wide expanse for the hundreds of thousands of people to cross.

Some have suggested that an earthquake or an avalanche caused the water to stop its flow. Regardless of the method God used, it was miraculous. The water stopped at exactly the right time and resumed its flow after the people got across (see Jos 4:18).

A throng of people a mile wide made their way down the steep riverbed and up the other side. Old men carefully found their way through the rocks. Children scampered down the deep cliffs picking up stones along the way. Mothers carried newborn infants. After what might have been several hours, everyone was safely over.

Sometimes we fear surrender to God, thinking He might make impossible demands. But whatever God commands us to do, He gives us the grace to do it. The impossible becomes possible when we choose to obey regardless of our fears.

God's miracles are thorough, right to the last detail. The people did not need to wipe their feet when they got to the other side. They crossed over on "dry ground."

One man from each of the tribes was to carry a stone out of the river to be used for a special memorial on the west bank. Joshua himself took twelve stones and set up a memorial in the riverbed (see Jos 4:9). Then suddenly the dry ground disappeared as a torrent of water came rushing down the riverbed once more.

Like Israel, we all walk a path we have never seen before. Each day is a new experience. A doctor may tell us we have cancer, a child may be injured in an accident, a teen may rebel against God. We may be unjustly fired from our job or discover that our investments have gone sour. We may have to face a hundred injustices from those we thought were our friends. In these and a thousand other circumstances we can be confident that we are not heading into the future alone.

Right at this moment events are taking place that will influence your future. Phone calls are being made, perhaps business transactions are on the horizon, and people, some of whom you have never met, are making decisions that will affect you. But God is supervising it all. He is there long before you are, making preparations.

I'm told that the average person loses between twenty and thirty hairs each day. Count the number of hairs in the sink after you wash your hair and be reminded, "But the very hairs of your head are all numbered" (Mt 10:30). God's computer is constantly in motion, keeping an accurate count. God is not only with us but has already traveled into our future to make preparations for our arrival.

"Do not fear, for I have redeemed you; I have called you by name; you are Mine! When you pass through the waters, I will be with you; and through the rivers, they will not overflow you" (Is 43:1-2).

What is the great lesson we learn from Israel? *No river is too crooked, no river is too deep, no river is too swift, but that God is able to help us through it.*

Got any rivers you think are uncrossable?
Got any mountains you can't tunnel through?
God specializes in things thought impossible.
He'll do what no other friend can do.

Only when the priests put their feet in the flowing river did a miracle take place. Though they began their journey with wet feet, by the time they got to the other side their feet were dry. God made a path where, humanly speaking, none could possibly be.

Many valleys flatten out once we take a step toward them, believing God for a miracle. And if no path appears, God is still there. "I will never desert you, nor will I ever forsake you" (Heb 13:5).

A yielded heart will take us through the river that leads to the promised land.

Chapter Six

Getting Ready for Battle
(Read Joshua 4–5)

And now for the basics.

Life is a classroom and our circumstances the curriculum. Unfortunately, there are no electives. Our exams take many forms, but our grade always depends on whether we have mastered the basics. All of life is relearning the essentials.

A pro football player was asked what he does to prepare for a play-off game. His answer was surprisingly simple: "I work on the fundamentals."

The struggle we faced this week, the fear that kept us from doing what we know we should—such tensions bring us back to the basics.

There are battles ahead. We face obstacles that are determined to keep us from being fruitful Christians. God is calling us to dig our roots into familiar soil so that we will not be swept away by the enemies that want to disrupt our souls.

We have learned that the corporate experiences of Israel are roughly parallel to the personal experience of each one of us. The geography of the Old Testament has symbolic meaning. All these things happened to them as examples for us.

Egypt represents the world. There the Israelites were in bondage to cruel managers who tried to kill the nation with hard work. Bondage to sin is even worse.

And how did God get them out of Egypt? Through the blood of the lamb. When that blood was sprinkled on the doorposts of the house, the angel of death passed over the house and the firstborn did not die. Through Christ, the Lamb of God, we are brought out of the slave market of sin to a new life.

The crossing of the Red Sea symbolizes the beginning of the Christian life. When we trust Christ as our Savior, we leave the world (Egypt) and become members of God's family. Thus we are, to use the word of Paul, "saved."

The desert experience represents periods of spiritual struggle and defeat; times of dissatisfaction with the Christian life, struggles with doubt and unfulfillment—this is the downside of Christian experience.

In the desert we hear rumors about the promised land, but we don't experience it yet. We hear people talking about victory over sin and the fullness of the Holy Spirit, but if we kept a diary it would be primarily a chronicle of repeated failure. We walk in circles. Though we are active, there is no evidence of spiritual progress. We would like to eat from the Lord's table, but there is a famine in our heart. We suspect that there is more to Christianity, but we don't know how to find it.

In the desert the Israelites spent much time complaining. In the evenings around the campfire two of the favorite topics were (1) Is the Lord with us or not? and (2) Should we anoint a new leader and return to Egypt?

In the desert we are very vulnerable to the world because we are so unfulfilled. We have not tasted to see that the Lord is good, so we turn this way and that, unable to find contentment with God. A heart nurtured in the desert does not have the strength to conquer Canaan.

The Jordan River represents a turning point. We die to our own plans and ambitions. Here we make a choice to face the enemies of our souls and take what God has promised us. We begin to be satisfied in Canaan and taste some of the fruit of the land.

Jordan is the point of no return. We set our faces to find fullness in Christ by closing the door behind us, resolved never to return to the world. We step across into Canaan and mean business. It's time the enemies that sap our psychological strength are identified and routed.

Interestingly, at this point in Israel's experience they had not yet encountered a single battle. Crossing the Jordan was a step of faith, but it was nothing in comparison to what lay before them. Drowning in the Jordan would have been much more tolerable than what they would face from the cruel Canaanites.

So before their first battle they had to regroup and become spiritually and emotionally prepared. Specifically, the stigma of forty years of defeat had to be put behind them so that they could march to Jericho with confidence.

The Israelites camped in Gilgal, just two miles from Jericho. The word Gilgal means *circle*. God took this word and invested it with new meaning: "Then the Lord said to Joshua, 'Today I have rolled away the reproach of Egypt from you.' So the name of that place is called Gilgal to this day" (Jos 5:9).

What, specifically, was "rolled away"? It was the disgrace Israel had endured in Egypt and in the desert. They were the people of God yet had suffered the humiliation of cringing before their enemies. They had the mentality of defeat rather than of victory. Their past failures had to be put away so that they could get on with being all that God had intended them to be.

One day I met a woman who had a tattoo on her arm. She explained to me that it was put there by her former boyfriend. She never did marry him; in fact, he became an abusive alcoholic. But the tattoo was still there. Though she was married to another man, every day of her life she had to be reminded of a previous painful relationship. In fact, her husband had to see it there too. How she wished she could get rid of that indelible reminder of her past!

You may have just such a tattoo on your soul—The stigma of divorce, moral impurity, addiction, or despair. If only the disgrace of past failure could be permanently put away!

God had to take this reproach away before the nation would be free to believe His promises. The stumbling blocks would have to be set aside before the walls would fall.

Despite the miracle of crossing the Jordan, the Israelites probably again felt like grasshoppers as they camped in the shadow of mighty Jericho. Here once and for all they would have to exchange the mentality of defeat for the mentality of victory. With God, they were giants about to crush grasshoppers.

With the reproach of the past gone, God exchanged the disgrace of defeat for the joy of victory. What happened at Gilgal?

Gilgal Was a Place of Remembrance

After everyone had crossed the dry riverbed, Joshua asked the twelve representatives to return to the riverbed, each one bringing a stone that would be used as a memorial. "Take for yourselves twelve men from the people, one man from each tribe, and command them, saying, 'Take up for yourselves twelve stones from here out of the middle of the Jordan, from the place where the priests' feet are standing firm, and carry them over with you, and lay them down in the lodging place where you will lodge tonight'" (Jos 4:2-3).

Joshua himself accompanied the representatives and made his own memorial right in the middle of the riverbed (see v. 9). He placed twelve stones there where they would never be seen again unless the Jordan were to become dry at some future date. The twelve visible stones at Gilgal represented the twelve invisible stones in the water.

I suppose I have seen a hundred memorials in my lifetime. In Washington there is the Lincoln Memorial, the Jefferson Memorial, the Washington Monument, and dozens of others to lesser heroes. In Russia I have seen memorials to Lenin, Marx, and Brezhnev. All of these are monuments to men who were believed to deserve high honor.

We need more monuments to God's faithfulness! We need constant reminders of what God has done in the past, to give us the assurance that He will be there when we need Him in the future.

Specifically, the rough monument of twelve stones was to be an object lesson for future generations. Joshua explained, "When your children ask their fathers in time to come, saying,

'What are these stones?' then you shall inform your children, saying, 'Israel crossed this Jordan on dry ground'" (vv. 21-22).

The memorial would point them east, the direction of the Jordan. They would recall the faithfulness of God in doing this mighty miracle.

It would also point them west, toward that land that needed to be conquered. Here was a prize to be won for God.

Israel could never return to the desert. If the nation were to retreat the stones would cry out against her. To make such a move would be to tear the throne of God from their hearts and throw it in the sand. Israel would have lost her credibility among the seven nations of the land. God would have been dishonored and future generations would have suffered.

The memorial was there to urge them to trust in God. If He could stop a river, He could subdue a city. If He had control over nature, He had control over brick and mortar.

Every Christian needs a memorial. We need something to point to that reminds us of God's faithfulness.

From time to time I record my spiritual experiences in a diary. I will write down the details of the trial I'm passing through. Recently, when I commemorated ten years of ministry at Moody Church, I sat down to read what I had written throughout the years. I was amazed at all the ups and downs; but it was a great encouragement to remember some obstacles and barriers I had successfully crossed with God's help.

One summer while on vacation I was filled with anxiety over a number of issues I faced here at the church. At the top of a page in my diary I wrote, MATTERS GIVEN FULLY OVER TO GOD. Beneath was a list of those concerns. Now, several years later, I just sat and smiled as I read them because God had taken care of all those issues long ago and the problems were not nearly as great as I had thought them to be. As one man said of himself, "My life has been filled with all kinds of emergencies that have never happened!"

The reproach of defeat is erased as we contemplate the faithfulness of God. Do you need courage to face the enemies of your soul? Refresh your memory about how God has led you in the past. Read the psalms that speak about the dependability of God in the past as a basis for future trust. Ask God to help you build a memorial to His faithfulness.

But Gilgal looked forward as well as backward. So God gave them some object lessons to whet their appetite for the new land.

A Place of Renewal

God now asked them to reinstitute two rites they had not practiced in the wilderness.

The first was circumcision. The males old enough to have participated in the Exodus had been circumcised, but not the younger generation. That was now done, in obedience to God (see Jos 5:2-9).

Why was this not practiced in the desert? Circumcision was given by God to Abraham as a sign of the covenant. God said that this rite would be a reminder that the people would be given the land and have posterity that would last forever.

But when you are in the desert you are not exactly thrilled about the promises of God. Who cares whether God promised you anything? Unfulfilled promises are useless and breed cynicism.

Second, there was the Passover. The nation had celebrated the Passover in Egypt the night they left to cross the Red Sea. Then they celebrated it again at Mount Sinai (see Nm 9:5). But they evidently had neglected it, so this also was revived at Gilgal (see Jos 5:10-11).

In the desert the Passover probably seemed out of place. It represented the faithfulness of God in getting them out from under the oppression of Pharaoh. But the people saw nothing worthy of celebration; they wanted to return to Egypt and regretted they had ever left! Camping in the hot sand for forty years did not exactly put them in a celebrating mood.

Gilgal also marked the first time God let the Israelites taste the produce of the land (see v. 12). At long last they began to experience the reason why God had brought them out of Egypt. God had promised to bring them into "a land of wheat and barley, of vines and fig trees and pomegranates, a land of olive oil and honey; a land where you shall eat food without scarcity, in which you shall not lack anything" (Dt 8:8-9). They began to realize that the stories they had heard were true after all. Yes, it was a land that flowed with milk and honey; there were corn and grain and cucumbers. The taste in their mouths was a tangible reminder that the land was just as God had said it would be.

If you are in the desert today, you need to be reminded of God's faithfulness. You also have to be renewed with God's promises. Once we have tasted the goodness of the Lord we will lose our appetite for the menu of the desert.

The question we must ask is: Why are we living in a desert when God has blessed us so richly in Christ?

My Father is rich in houses and lands,
He holdeth the wealth of the world in His hands!
Of rubies and diamonds, of silver and gold,
His coffers are full, He has riches untold.
I'm a child of the King, a child of the King:
With Jesus my Savior, I'm a child of the King.

What promises of God have we allowed to slip through our fingers?

A Place of Realization

There was still an important question that needed an answer: Who would be in charge of the military campaign against Jericho? Joshua needed some assurance that he was under the control of someone mightier than he. Unexpectedly he learned where he fit in the military chain of command.

That night, with all of these exciting developments whirling in his mind, Joshua decided to take a walk to Jericho to see the city for himself. No doubt he was planning strategy to take the city. His exact thoughts, of course, we do not know.

Suddenly a soldier appeared with a sword drawn in His hand. Joshua didn't recognize the warrior, and asked, "Are You for us or for our adversaries?" (Jos 5:13). If this were an Israelite, Joshua wanted to know what he was doing here, since it was past curfew. If he were a Canaanite, Joshua was ready to fight.

But the man didn't answer the question. He was not on the side of the enemy, nor did He affirm that He was on Joshua's side. "No, rather I indeed come now as captain of the host of the Lord" (v. 14).

Who was this? Bible scholars throughout the centuries have called this a "theophany," that is, a manifestation of God—specifically a manifestation of Christ. This was Christ appearing as a man fourteen hundred years before He appeared as a baby in Bethlehem. This was God in human form. Little wonder Joshua bowed in worship.

How did He come? As captain of "the host of the Lord." The Hebrew word *host* means "army." He was captain of the armies of God. He represented unseen armies, angels who were under His command to fight for the people of God.

As twentieth-century rationalists we often do not appreciate the direct connection between physical and spiritual battles. That is not just a contemporary problem but an ancient one.

Consider this scenario: One day a prophet named Elisha was sitting with his servant near the town of Dothan in northern Israel. The Syrian army had surrounded the city to capture Elisha. The servant was terrified, but Elisha assured him, "Do not fear, for those who are with us are more than those who are with them." Then the prophet prayed "and the Lord opened the servant's eyes, and he saw; and behold, the mountain was full of horses and chariots of fire all around Elisha" (2 Kgs 6:16-17).

If God were to touch our eyes so that we could see the spiritual realm, we would be astounded at the activity swirling around us every minute. Our world is populated with angels and demons who are extensions of the activity of God and the devil.

Christ said in Gethsemane that there were tens of thousands of angels ready to deliver Him if He but gave them the word. Angels are "ministering spirits sent forth to minister to those who will inherit salvation" (Heb 1:14, NKJV).

The battles we sometimes explain as natural phenomena may really be extensions of spiritual battles. Yes, even taking Jericho was not just a matter of military strategy but a matter of spiritual combat. The victory won by Joshua in the physical realm would only be the result of a fiercer battle in the spiritual realm.

People often wonder how we can tell whether a problem is demonic or a struggle with our own sinful nature. Sometimes Satan's activity is difficult to detect because he works through the weakness and sins of the flesh to accomplish his purposes. But we can be quite certain that every spiritual battle involves conflict with the hosts of darkness. The extent of the demonic activity may vary, but the fact that we are in conflict with these spirit beings is undeniable.

Joshua needed to learn that he would have to pay more attention to his own spiritual life (and that of the nation) than to military strategy. For if his mind was centered on obedience to God, the military challenge would be solved.

He would have to learn that taking charge of a city is easier than taking charge of one's own heart. The rest of the Book of Joshua proves a basic principle: *The state of the heart within determines the result of the battle without.* With characteristic wisdom Luther said, "I fear my own heart more than I do all the cardinals and the pope."

Notice that the man with the sword did not respond directly to Joshua's question. He did not say which side He was on! For when God walks on the scene, He does not come to take sides. *He comes to take over.* Joshua now realized that the matter was out of his hands. God was not at his side to help him; God was ahead of him, asking only that he follow. It was not a matter of *sides* but *sovereignty*. The battle was not his but the Lord's.

Think of how Joshua must have slept that night, knowing that God was in control!

When God takes over He puts an end to our own plans.

We end manipulation, for God has taken over.
We end anxiety, for God has taken over.
We end pride, for God has taken over.
We end self-exaltation, for God has taken over.
We end criticism of others, for God has taken over.

God is well able to take away the reproach of failure and substitute for it the mentality of victory! That tattoo on our souls can be removed by the touch of God.

Let God roll your failures away and get you ready for your biggest challenge.

Jericho is just over the next hill!

Chapter Seven

Your First Big Fight
(Read Joshua 6)

There is a story about two men, both seriously ill, in the same room of a great hospital. One of them, as part of his treatment, was allowed to sit up in bed for an hour in the afternoon to drain fluid from his lungs, and his bed was next to the window.

But the other man had to spend all his time flat on his back; and both of them had to be quiet and still. There could be no reading, no radio, and certainly no television. They talked for hours about their wives, their children, their homes, their jobs.

Every afternoon when the man in the bed next to the window was propped up for an hour he would pass the time by describing what he could see outside. And the other man began to live for those hours.

The window apparently overlooked a park with a lake, where there were ducks and swans, children throwing them bread and sailing model boats, and young lovers walking hand in hand; there were flowers and stretches of grass, games of softball, people taking their ease in the sunshine, and in the distance a fine view of the city skyline.

The man on his back would listen to all of this, enjoying

every minute: how a child was saved from falling into the lake, how beautiful the girls were in their summer dresses, and then an exciting ball game or a boy playing with his puppy. It got to the point where the man lying on his back could almost see what was happening outside.

As the days progressed the man on his back became resentful that he could not be propped up next to the window to see all these sights for himself. He brooded, lost sleep, and became more angry at his plight.

One morning the man next to the window was found dead; his body was taken quietly away. As soon as it seemed decent the man asked if he could be moved to the bed next to the window. And when they moved him they tucked him in, and made him quite comfortable, and left him alone to be quiet and still.

The minute they left, he propped himself up on one elbow, painfully and laboriously, and looked out the window.

It faced a *blank wall!*

Every one of us, sooner or later, will find that we are boxed in, without a door or window. A blank wall will appear across our spiritual pathway that will be difficult, if not impossible, to remove. There it stands to taunt us, and, yes, to haunt us. When we think about conquering it, it seems to shout, "I dare you to try!"

Joshua stood a few miles from Jericho, facing the greatest challenge of his career. Archeologists tell us that the walls were perhaps twelve feet thick and twenty to thirty feet high. Soldiers probably stood on the ramparts to report on troop movements and to make sure that no one would have the courage to scale the walls with ladder and rope. Behind those walls was a formidable war machine that was enough to make the bravest soldier shudder. To penetrate this fortification and rout the enemy was more than could be expected of the ill-equipped Israelite army.

As Joshua stared at these huge walls, he had the faith to see through them. While many of his terrified soldiers saw only brick and mortar, Joshua was able to see the glory of God. The eye of faith is not blinded by circumstances; no matter how tall the walls, God is taller still.

Now that the reproach of Israel had been wiped away at Gilgal, the nation was ready for its first all-out war. The people could believe again.

As already indicated, Jericho figuratively represents Satan's opposition when we begin to get serious with God. When we cross our Jordan through submission and faith, we are immediately headed for discouragement. We encounter an enemy who seems larger with each passing moment. We meet those walls whose foundations are deep and which seem to ascend into the heavens.

Your Jericho may be your background of abuse, rejection, or emotional pain. It may be the disintegration of your marriage, a financial collapse, or immorality. Whatever, it stands between you and your walk with God.

God is as ready to help us in our need as He was to help Joshua in his. Winning against our enemies is a gift from God, but it must be received with determination and faith.

God begins by giving Joshua a promise: "See, I have given Jericho into your hand, with its king and the valiant warriors" (Jos 6:2). Here is the same promise given earlier, repeated for this specific situation.

Incredibly, God again puts the promise in the past tense: "I *have* given Jericho into your hand." The Israelites might have objected, pointing to the massive walls and closed gates. What could God mean when He said that the city was already theirs?

But God often speaks in the past tense about events that are yet future. Even Isaiah the prophet, six hundred years before Christ, wrote about the Crucifixion as if it had already taken place (see Is 53:5). The apostle Paul speaks of God as one "who gives life to the dead and calls into being that which does not exist" (Rom 4:17).

Just as Israel was given the land by God as a present possession, so we today have been blessed "with every spiritual blessing in the heavenly places in Christ" (Eph 1:3). Right now, in the middle of all of our defeats and victories, we have it all!

The promise is very specific: The king of Jericho and his warriors would be overcome. The *what* was clear, the *how* was not.

Once again, Joshua was forced to trust God to do a miracle. God gave him detailed instructions as to what he and his armies were to do, but he knew nothing about what *God* was going to do. Obedience does not mean that we understand how and when God will work.

God's instructions were: "And you shall march around the city, all the men of war circling the city once. You shall do so for six days. Also seven priests shall carry seven trumpets of rams' horns before the ark; then on the seventh day you shall march around the city seven times, and the priests shall blow the trumpets. And it shall be that when they make a long blast with the ram's horn, and when you hear the sound of the trumpet, all the people shall shout with a great shout; and the wall of the city will fall down flat, and the people will go up every man straight ahead" (Jos 6:3-5).

Obviously, these instructions do not apply to us literally, for our Jerichos are quite different from the ancient city three miles west of the Jordan. But we do have some important principles that will help us to understand how our particular strongholds are to be captured.

We March Defenselessly

Yes, Israel had some men of war, but they were vastly outnumbered by the enemy. As already pointed out, their weapons were inferior and their strategy strained credulity. As Kent Hughes says, "The uniform witness of military history is that the foe is conquered by force. City walls are cleared by bombardment. Then they are scaled by ladder and rope. Gates are destroyed by battering rams. Troops are taken by the sword. Cities do not fall before mystics making bad music on rams' horns" *(Living on the Cutting Edge,* Westchester, Ill.: Crossway, '74).

The lopsided advantages of the Canaanites were clear to all. Even apart from the inferior weaponry of the Israelites, the odds always go to the army that is entrenched behind a fortification. We've already learned that it is much more difficult to capture an enemy position than it is to defend one.

Even today, we march with God alone as our shield. "Behold, I send you out as sheep in the midst of wolves," Christ said to His disciples, "therefore be shrewd as serpents, and innocent as doves" (Mt 10:16). Unless God defends us, we are doomed.

Joshua's experience at Jericho is a reminder that no fortification is too strong for God to overcome. We must march with confidence that God will give us the right strategy to overcome the enemy. Blessed are those who can see beyond their walls to God.

We March Patiently

For six days the Israelites marched around the city without any evidence that they were close to victory. Even as they began the journey on the seventh day, they appeared no closer to their goal. Imagine the conversations the preceding night as the children asked why this weary and boring routine had to be repeated. Despite all the marching, the walls did not become smaller, the enemy did not become weaker, and the Israelites did not become stronger. Joshua could not offer a shred of evidence for obeying God.

An explorer, Fridtjof Nansen, was lost with one companion in the Arctic wastes. By miscalculation they ran out of all their supplies. They ate their dogs, the dogs' harnesses, the whale oil for their lamps. Nansen's companion lay down to die, but Nansen told himself, "I can take one more step." As he plodded heavily through the bitter cold, step after step, suddenly he came upon an American expedition that had been sent out to find him.

We do not know what God might do when we take that extra step. Dr. Alan Redpath has suggested that many people don't see answers to their prayers because they have stopped at round twelve in the conquest of their personal Jericho! We may be doing all the right things and must simply keep doing them! The enemy may fall into our hands soon.

We March Silently

There was a time to shout, but there was also a time to be silent. The Israelites could not even encourage themselves with shouts of victory. Most likely the Canaanites shouted cat-calls over the walls, jeering the hapless troops below. But they were not to retaliate in kind. They were to remain silent and see the glory of the Lord.

"Come, behold the works of the Lord, who has wrought desolations in the earth. He makes wars to cease to the end of the earth; He breaks the bow and cuts the spear in two; He burns the chariots with fire. Cease striving and know that I am God; I will be exalted among the nations, I will be exalted in the earth. The Lord of hosts is with us; the God of Jacob is our stronghold" (Ps 46:8-11).

Let us be still and know that the Lord is God.

We March Unitedly

The people were well organized as they made their journey around Jericho. First came the men of war, then seven priests followed, carrying seven trumpets, and behind them came the ark of the covenant. The people followed this procession as it wound its way around the city.

This was not to be a victory for Joshua alone. This was "people power"; or more accurately, the power of a united nation in dependence on God. Together they would live or die.

If you are confronting a particularly strong Jericho, you cannot do it alone. The body of Christ is to function in unity; there is spiritual strength in numbers. If those numbers are wholly committed to God, there is reason to believe that Jerichos will have to tumble. We must share our burdens with others who can make them lighter, others who understand the power of intercessory prayer. And when one believer stumbles, another must be there to cushion the fall.

We March Expectantly

As they walked around the city for the seventh time on the seventh day, God did a miracle. "So the people shouted, and the priests blew the trumpets; and it came about, when the people heard the sound of the trumpet, that the people shouted with a great shout and the wall fell down flat, so that the people went up into the city, every man straight ahead, and they took the city" (Jos 6:20).

Those huge walls collapsed for one reason: The captain of the host of the Lord spoke and His invisible armies pushed them over! Huge mounds of rubble and dried mud slid down the side of the hill and became the stepping stones that the Israelites used to go into the city and destroy the terrified populace.

The Israelites themselves were astonished at what God had done. God prefers to keep His plans a secret; we don't have to know what He is going to do until He actually does it. Our responsibility is to walk in faith, knowing that there may be a surprise around the corner.

We March Triumphantly

Though the walls of Jericho came down, the battle was not over. Not only did the people have to be exterminated, but all of their possessions had to be burned. Only the silver and gold were kept for the treasury of the Lord. Everything else went up in smoke.

Many people are troubled because God commanded Joshua to exterminate everyone (except Rahab, of course). However, we must remember that these people were extremely depraved and their cup of wickedness was now filled to the brim (see Gn 15:16). They were so corrupt that a pure faith could not coexist with them. Their idolatry would infect the nation of Israel. God was serving notice that *sin is extremely contagious.*

Think of the temptation the people experienced, the temptation to keep some of the oxen, clothes, and utensils for their own enrichment. They could not understand why God told them to destroy what was good. In subsequent battles they would be able to keep some of the spoils for themselves, but in this first military victory God wanted to leave them with an object lesson: Sin spreads so easily that even the items that belonged to the Canaanites should be burned.

There are some powerful concluding lessons we can learn from Israel's experience:

1. Our basic battles in life are spiritual, not physical, emotional,

or even psychological. To the casual observer, it would appear as if the battle of Jericho was a conflict between two visible armies. But it was actually a battle between two *in*visible armies, the hosts of the Lord and the hosts of darkness.

This explains why our greatest challenge is to enlist Christ's resources to fight our battles. The real conflict is not only between husbands and wives, parents and children, employers and employees—these conflicts only mirror battles in the spiritual world. Of course there still would be conflicts in the world if Satan did not exist, for we have a corrupt, sinful nature that is constantly vying to have its own way. But the presence of Satan and his evil spirits causes manageable conflicts to become unmanageable. Satan takes a skirmish and turns it into an all-out war.

Behind our visible Jericho is an invisible foe that can be overcome only by obedience to God and faith in His promises.

2. Whether we win or lose depends on our focus. If we stand and stare at the walls, they will only appear greater, more fortified, and more impossible to overcome. If we focus on God, those walls will turn into windows through which we can see the glory of God.

I have often been a wall-watcher. I have spent time analyzing my walls; I have studied their foundations, measured their height, and estimated their weight. Yet, for all my investigation, the walls do not budge.

During World War II there was a younger soldier who took his new bride to California, where he was stationed for more training. Then he was taken away for two weeks and his young bride was overcome by loneliness, heat, and the primitive living conditions. She wrote to her mother, saying that she was unable to take it any longer. Her mother wrote back and included these two lines:

Two men sit in prison bars;
One sees mud, the other stars.

That couplet transformed the young woman's attitude. She began to see God in her circumstances and looked for opportunities to make the best of her situation.

To see the beauty of God beyond a blank wall is the privilege of every one of us. Some do it better than others, but all of us must see beyond our prison to God.

To *glance* at our walls but *gaze* at God is the first step in overcoming our personal Jericho. "Through God we shall do valiantly, and it is He who will tread down our adversaries" (Ps 60:12).

It's not where you *are* but what you *see* that really matters.

Chapter Eight

The High Cost of Hidden Sin
(Read Joshua 7)

Almost always when a tire has a blowout the cause can be traced to a weakness in the tire that has been developing for months. Those weaknesses are difficult to detect and even more difficult to predict. Yet it may be a small, almost invisible crack that becomes the cause of a major accident.

Spiritual and moral failure have their causes too. And like a microscopic crack in a tire, these causes may be near impossible to pinpoint. Unless we take the early warning signals seriously, we will find ourselves in a spiritual wreck.

But how do we uncover the causes of defeat? Especially when we are such masters at skillfully hiding these sins, even from ourselves!

That's why counseling is such a challenge. A person struggles with depression: Is the cause physical, psychological, spiritual, or a combination of the three? Sometimes the answer may be clear, at other times we may never know.

Another person lives with irrational fears. Where did these fears originate? And if we can uncover the cause, what is the cure? Similar challenges come our way when we are confronted with those involved in immorality, drugs, anger, or the inability to form close relationships. These and a hundred other personal problems need analysis with the hope of finding both the cause and the cure.

Let's broaden the problem to include the ills of our society. To what can we trace our economic woes, the political paralysis that makes our leaders turn away from high moral leadership? Why is the killing of unborn children so widely accepted in the face of overwhelming evidence that we are killing human beings? Why are we losing the drug war?

The story of Achan illustrates how secular man is often unable to uncover the causes of personal or social ruin. There are spiritual forces at work that defy the analysis of men who do not understand the ways of God.

Visualize the events of Joshua 7: Joshua sends some spies to Ai to assess the strength of this city, small in comparison to Jericho. They return with good news: "Do not let all the people go up; only about two or three thousand men need go up to Ai; do not make all the people toil up there, for they are few" (v. 3).

Bolstered by this optimistic report, Joshua sends about three thousand men to capture the city. Victory is virtually assured in light of the weakness of the enemy. Yet surprisingly, not only is Joshua's army forced to retreat but thirty-six men are lost in the process. A surefire victory backfires and results in a humiliating defeat.

Stop for a moment and ask: How would a military man analyze the cause of the defeat? Various explanations might be given. The Israelite army should have used better weapons or they had poor strategy or perhaps they simply underestimated the number of men needed. And the list of explanations could go on.

Interestingly, Joshua learned that the cause of defeat had nothing to do with military matters. The reason was that one man had disobeyed God back at the siege of Jericho by taking some gold, silver, and a coat, and hiding them in his tent! On the surface such an explanation seems absurd. What possible relationship could there be between a petty act of thievery and thirty-six dead men on the battlefield? The two events seem totally unrelated.

However, God makes relationships that do not fit our neat pattern of analysis. *Spiritual forces are often connected with physical events in ways that are beyond our understanding.* There is an interconnectedness that must be accepted if we are to understand ourselves and the events around us.

Let's consider three relationships that should help us pinpoint the cause of some failures.

The Relationships Between People

We read, "But the sons of Israel acted unfaithfully in regard to the things under the ban, for Achan, the son of Carmi, the son of Zabdi, the son of Zerah, from the tribe of Judah, took some of the things under the ban, therefore the anger of the Lord burned against the sons of Israel" (Jos 7:1).

If I had been of the tribe of Simeon I might have objected, complaining that I had nothing to do with Achan's sin. What he did was his business alone. Why should I have to suffer for what someone from another tribe did?

However reasonable such thinking might be, the fact is that the entire nation was in some way involved in this incident.

Indeed, it was the whole nation that felt the sting of the defeat of the army at Ai. No person's sin is ever his business alone; it always affects others.

In the giving of the Law, the Lord said, "I, the Lord your God, am a jealous God, visiting the iniquity of the fathers on the children, on the third and the fourth generations of those who hate Me, but showing lovingkindness to thousands, to those who love Me and keep My commandments" (Ex 20:5-6).

Parents affect their children for good or ill. The influence of the family network is so powerful that we all bear the stamp of our upbringing. Yes, parents can bless us or curse us; they can motivate us to godliness or discourage us from spiritual development. Often the sins of the father are perpetuated in the lives of his children. The interconnectedness of families has been established by God.

A woman came to me seeking counsel regarding her teenage daughter who was into drugs and immorality. My first question was, "How are you and your husband getting along?" It turned out that they had recently separated because of marital infidelity. What she didn't realize was that her daughter's way-wardness could be traced to the example and influence of her parents.

Children who were reared in dysfunctional families must be taught that God is able to break these negative influences. But even then, these parental influences can crop up unexpectedly, so a child must guard against special temptations and weaknesses. No parent can say that his or her sin is no one else's business. No matter how secret the sin might be, its effects spill over into the lives of others.

Of course the same applies to children reared in homes

where the parents or other relatives have been involved in demonic activity. Demonic influences are often passed on. One day Christ was asked to cast out a demon from a child who was being tormented by evil spirits (see Mk 9:18). When the father was asked how long this had been going on, he replied, "From childhood" (v. 21). Clearly that child had not committed a sin to invite the spirit. Likely the older relatives had been involved in occult activity.

Thankfully, Christ is able to break the destructive influences of family relationships. Adults cannot blame their failures on their pasts, for God says, "The son will not bear the punishment for the father's iniquity; the righteousness of the righteous will be upon himself, and the wickedness of the wicked will be upon himself" (Ez 18:20). Nonetheless, family influences can be powerful. Families have not just physical but also spiritual connections. No man lives unto himself or dies unto himself.

The same is true with the body of Christ. An individual Christian may think that his coldness of heart affects no one else. But there is no such thing as a believer who carries no influence with the whole body.

Visualize a bucket of water heated to, say, 100 degrees. Each of us is given a cup of water to pour into the larger container. Whether our cup is hot, cold, or lukewarm, we will affect the temperature of the entire bucket.

Individuals within a church may grow spiritually even if the majority of the members are carnal. But the detrimental effect of those who are spiritually cold will surely be felt. Some of the organs of a human body can be healthy while others are sick, but the function of the body will be impaired. No part of the body can claim autonomy since every cell either contributes or detracts from a body's performance.

When Achan sinned by stealing what had been specifically banned by God, the Lord said, "Israel has sinned." The whole nation felt the sting of one man's disobedience.

Perhaps there is a small (or large) crack in my life or yours that can be traced to our family influence, or perhaps we have been adversely affected by the weakness of our church family. We must ask God to remove these detrimental effects and strengthen our lives through repentance (if we are tolerating sin) and firm discipline. Or perhaps the crack is entirely my fault. Either way, I must make sure that it is healed.

A small crack can produce a big blowout.

The Relationship Among Sins

Eventually Achan was forced to come clean, to confess his sin and publicly tell the whole story: "When I saw among the spoil a beautiful mantle from Shinar and two hundred shekels of silver and a bar of gold fifty shekels in weight, then I coveted them and took them; and behold, they are concealed in the earth inside my tent with the silver underneath it" (Jos 7:21).

The sin began secretly. He *coveted* the coat and the money that were left behind in the destruction of Jericho. Then he *stole* them and *hid* them. The sin that began in his heart soon involved his whole body. And it eventually affected his whole family.

When we tolerate sin we set in motion a domino effect that can ultimately lead to our ruin. The alcoholic saw only the enjoyment of the first drink; he did not foresee the destruction of his family. He could not predict the disgrace and bondage that would eventually ruin his life. The same goes for sins such as immorality, covetousness, and deceit.

When we allow one sin to have free reign in our lives it is like burning incense in a dormitory. No matter how many towels are pushed under the door, within a short while it can be smelled in the hallways. Soon the aroma wafts into the elevator and even onto the next floor. Similarly, there is no way that sin can be neatly confined.

Somewhere I read about three laws of sowing and reaping. Briefly stated, they are: (1) We always reap what we sow. Paul puts it this way, "Do not be deceived, God is not mocked; for whatever a man sows, this he will also reap. For the one who sows to his own flesh shall from the flesh reap corruption, but the one who sows to the Spirit shall from the Spirit reap eternal life" (Gal 6:7-8). If we sow sensuality, we will reap it; if we are covetous, we will reap the bitter fruits of greed that accompany it.

Then (2) You always reap more than you sow. One grain of wheat can produce perhaps fifty kernels. Sin brings consequences far in excess of the sin committed. David would never have dreamed that one act of immorality with Bathsheba would eventually lead to the disintegration of his family and disgrace to himself and his kingdom. Sin, like a forest fire, begins with a single match, then spreads in unpredictable and haphazard ways. We definitely do reap more than we sow.

(3) Finally, we reap in a different season than we sow. This is what makes sin so deceptive: The immediate consequences appear to be minimal and perhaps even invisible. If you planted

an acorn and returned to the spot every day for a month, it would appear to be dead. We may hide our sins and even control the consequences, but only for a time.

This explains why some sins are so difficult to be rid of; their power is augmented by other vices that are tolerated in the soul. Secret sins send roots deep into the soil of the heart, and eventually these roots break forth with awesome power and destruction.

The Relationship in Judgment

The story of how Achan was identified clearly exemplifies the lengths to which we will go to keep our shameful sins hidden. Joshua was commanded by God to find the culprit by casting lots.

First of all the tribe of Judah "was taken," that is, the lot indicated that the thief was from that particular tribe. Then the family of the Zerahites was identified. Then the lot began to zero in on the household of Achan, and he was finally pointed out as the one who had disobeyed the instructions of the Lord (see Jos 7:16-21).

Put yourself in Achan's shoes. You know right well that you are going to be found out. You know God will use the lot to let Joshua know who is to blame for this sin. Why not spare Joshua the hassle and go public with your confession? Why hold the nation in suspense when you know that you are going to have to face the inevitable?

Logical though that sounds, you and I probably would have done the same thing. We would have held out as long as we possibly could. The shame of exposure is so powerful that we would give anything to buy just a few more moments of sentimental hypocrisy. None of us enjoy having our secret sins exposed. That's why lying and deception accompany all other sins.

In his book *People of the Lie* (New York: Simon & Schuster, 1983, 75), M. Scott Peck speaks of some people as being particularly adept at concealing evil. These people, he says, are "Utterly dedicated to preserving their self-image of perfection, they are unceasingly engaged in the effort to maintain the appearance of moral purity. They worry about this a great deal. They dress well, go to work on time, pay their taxes, and outwardly seem to live lives that are beyond reproach."

Peck continues, "The words 'image' and 'appearance' and 'outwardly' are crucial to understanding the morality of the evil. While they seem to lack any motivation to be good, they intensely desire to appear good. Their 'goodness' is all on the level of pretense. It is, in effect, a lie. That is why they are people of 'the lie.'"

Actually, the lie Peck speaks of is designed not so much to deceive others as to deceive oneself. These "people of the lie" cannot or will not tolerate the pain of self-reproach. Even death is more bearable than allowing truth to come out.

The pain of self-reproach has kept many a person from coming to God for forgiveness and acceptance. Many live a secret life of evil, unwilling to be exposed at any cost.

Parenthetically, let me say that when the power of God comes to a community during periods of revival, the conviction of sin is so excruciating that people are willing to finally be honest with one another regardless of the humiliation. *The misery of concealed sin becomes so powerful that individuals give up their pride-filled deceptions and do whatever is necessary to rectify their relationships with God and one another.* They return stolen merchandise, confess their bitterness toward one another, and make restitution for their past failures. The pain of honesty is preferable to the pain of concealed sin.

Achan and his family, and even their donkeys, were stoned to death in the sight of all Israel. Then they were burned with fire, and a heap of stones was placed over the ashes. Thankfully, the Lord's anger was thereby assuaged (see vv. 24-26).

Again we might complain that it wasn't fair for Achan's family to be judged with him. After all, they were not to blame for his sins. Perhaps they had been accomplices, knowing full well what he was hiding in the tent. Whole families often do have to participate in the judgment of their parents' sins, at least in this life. A child of an alcoholic mother is born with deformities, or an innocent wife receives the deadly disease of AIDS from her immoral husband.

We've learned that our lives are so interconnected that it is impossible to exempt ourselves from the effects of other people's sins. Just as we often are blessed because of the lives of others, so we also are affected by their sins.

The lesson of Achan is that *the cause of our failures may often lie outside the realm of our initial investigation.* We may think that our anger stems from our uncaring boss, when the root cause may be traced back to our hostility toward God for allowing us to be abused at an early age. The alcoholic may be trying to drown his feelings of guilt; the drug addict may be trying to cope with the pain of rejection. The root of sin bears fruit in many different forms; it grows under a variety of labels.

One lesson Joshua learned from "the Achan affair" was that prayer can be hindered by unconfessed sin. After the defeat of Ai, Joshua poured out his soul to God, even questioning why God had bothered to bring the nation over the Jordan if He was going to fail them now. The Lord responded, "Rise up! Why is it that you have fallen on your face? Israel has sinned, and they have also transgressed My covenant.... Therefore the sons of Israel cannot stand before their enemies; they turn their backs before their enemies, for they have become accursed. I will not be with you any more unless you destroy the things under the ban from your midst" (vv. 10-12).

Unconfessed sin can hinder our prayers. A woman who was contemplating suicide told me she called on God for hours at a time but the heavens were silent. A few questions revealed that she was intensely bitter toward a former husband who had betrayed her. That root of anger had grown into other sins that she had been unwilling to confess and forsake. She received help from God when instead of praying, "Lord, help me!" she now prayed, "Lord, *forgive* me!"

One day a friend wanted to earnestly pray for his daughter who was about to be married. As he knelt in prayer, it was as if God said to him, "Henry, don't bother praying!" That struck him as strange, given the fact that God so clearly commands us to pray! The Holy Spirit brought to his mind that years earlier he had cheated on a term paper while attending college. This sin which had remained hidden was now interfering with his fellowship with God. Only when he returned to the university to confess his sin did he have freedom in his relationship with God and strength in his praying.

Hidden sin has done more to weaken our spiritual lives

than all the pressures of life we often complain about. Hidden sin has sapped our energy, diminished our witness, and ruined our families. If all the hidden sins in our lives were suddenly exposed, we would be shocked, wondering how we ever made it as far as we have, spiritually.

Finally, hidden sin *makes it impossible for us to claim the promises of God.* Try as we might, we cannot believe God for the help we seek as long as we avoid the pain of humble confession. The thirty-six men who died on the battlefield near Ai did not conquer the territory they walked on, notwithstanding the promise of God. Despite their apparent confidence, God allowed them to be crushed like grasshoppers.

Luther said that all sin is contempt of God. When we deliberately sin, we are saying that we know better than God what is best. No one who disagrees with God can expect to receive the strength He promises.

The most important part of us is that part which no one sees except God. Secret sin leads to public failure. We need to ask God to search our hearts to see if there are hidden sins we have not been willing to face.

"He who conceals his transgressions will not prosper, but he who confesses and forsakes them will find compassion" (Prv 28:13).

Even unseen cracks in a tire can cause a blowout.

Chapter Nine

Taking Charge Over the Enemy
(Read Joshua 8)

Christianity has always been at war with its culture. We are at odds with the world, for its values are in conflict with God's revealed will. We are at war with the flesh, those sinful desires that must be checked lest they destroy us. We are at war with the devil, a malicious and cruel being who seeks our destruction.

The war with Satan is largely invisible, for we are not involved in physical combat. During World War II many enemy troop movements were undetected, but theoretically at least it was possible to trace their whereabouts. Not so with Satan. We cannot see where he or his evil spirits are; we cannot discern their movements from place to place, though we have often felt their presence pressing on our minds or have confronted them in people who are under their evil control. We appear to be at a disadvantage, for Satan can see us though we cannot see him. But, as we shall see, this does not hinder us from winning victories for God.

Like all wars, this one is based on the principle of deception. Satan always comes to us like a friend, never an enemy. The power of temptation lies in the message that if we give in to it, we will be happy. Thus sin is always presented as something good rather than destructive.

Five hundred years before the time of Christ, Sun Tzu wrote a classic book on warfare, entitled *The Art of War* (New York: Oxford Press, 1973). The military principles he teaches are the very strategies Satan uses against us. Of the opponent Sun Tzu writes, "Keep him under a strain and wear him down" (p. 68); "If he doubles his strength, divide him" (p. 80); "When near, make it appear that you are far away, when far away, that you are near" (p. 66).

Here is another principle that makes good military sense: "The enemy must not know where I intend to give battle, for if he does not know where I intend to give battle, he must prepare in a great many places, those I have to fight in any one place will be few" (p. 98). The warning is clear: Since we don't know when and where the attack will come, we have to be ready everywhere.

Even we as Christians often feel powerless to challenge the lies that are widely believed. Virtually every step downward is portrayed as a step upward. Under the banner of progress we see moral and spiritual decay all around us. We are at war, and routing the enemy is no easy task.

Joshua was a military strategist who knew how to bring the enemy into submission. He had the good sense to know that wars are not won by fond wishes but by hard work and planning. Yes, and there is danger too.

The more spiritually aware we become, the more conscious we will be that our private and public battles involve unseen powers ruled by Satan. Paul reminded us that our battles are not with flesh and blood; there is much more to spiritual conflict than meets the eye.

Name your stronghold: anger, bitterness, addiction,

immorality— these are the enemies of the soul that must be overcome. These forces and a host of others like them are strengthened by the power of Satan.

Joshua had just experienced the most humiliating defeat of his career. The cause was hidden sin. Joshua had neglected to seek the face of God before he attempted his military venture. Quite possibly the Lord would have revealed to him that there was sin in the camp and he would not have sent his troops to Ai.

But now all that was behind him. He marched to the very city that had defeated him. And this time, he captured it to the glory of God.

Let's analyze the principles of warfare that enabled Joshua to finally be victorious at Ai. And as we do, let us let Ai represent our battle with Satan. Think of your area of conflict with the devil and how you can use these principles to overcome him.

The Relationship Between Purity and Power

Joshua had just learned the far-reaching consequences of hidden sin. He was still mourning the thirty-six men who had been killed on the battlefield because of Achan. He had become more aware of the subtle deceitfulness of human nature—and was determined to stress the need for personal holiness among the people.

Try as we might, we cannot separate purity and power. Now that the nation had been cleansed of its sin, the promise of God could again be applied to the conflict at hand.

Perhaps Joshua was still fearful, thinking that some other Israelite may have concealed serious sin. So the Lord repeated His promise: "Do not fear or be dismayed. Take all the people of war with you and arise, go up to Ai; see, I have given into your hand the king of Ai, his people, his city, and his land" (Jos 8:1).

Have you ever had to return to a place of defeat? There is a story told by Arthur Gossip about a boy fighting in World War I who because of illness was unable to face the enemy and was court-martialed for it. But despite the incident, the colonel continued to treat the boy with friendliness and respect. A few weeks later in a particularly tight corner the colonel put the boy in command of the very company with whom he had failed. In a few grim days of fighting the boy won one honor after another along with a promotion. "What else could I do?" the boy said to Arthur Gossip, "I failed him and he still trusted me!"

That's how Joshua must have felt as he made plans to conquer the city which had so recently defeated him. God trusted him to return to the place of defeat and turn it into a place of victory.

With Achan's sin behind him, Joshua now looked to the future. His dependence on God did not lead to complacency, expecting victory without effort or risk. He saw that there is a point at which the promises of God and human effort converge, working together to produce the desired outcome. He mobilized his troops and followed a careful strategy.

Fighting Together, Not Alone

If there was any thought in Joshua's mind that he would use the same methodology to conquer Ai as had been successfully used in Jericho, that mistaken notion was quickly dispelled. The Lord now told him to "set an ambush for the city behind it" (Jos 8:2). There would be no parade around the walls, no blaring of the trumpets.

Let me outline the strategy Joshua used to capture Ai. He chose men to make a fifteen-mile journey at night, going around the city and camping on its east side. They would lie in ambush until needed.

Then he sent men to the east, stationed between Ai and the neighboring city of Bethel. They were there to make sure that no reinforcements would come from this other town, perhaps five miles away. Ai would be isolated and would have to fight alone.

He then came up against the south side of Ai in broad daylight. When the troops of Ai took chase, Joshua and his army fled, appearing to be terrified by the onslaught. The forces of Ai came on the attack, convinced that victory was at hand. Then, with the city emptied of its warriors, the Israelites who were lying in ambush in the valley swarmed into the city, killing the inhabitants and setting it on fire.

Meanwhile the troops of Ai looked back and saw the billows of smoke ascending to the sky and knew they had been tricked. As they ran back to their city they were met by the Israelite soldiers who had stormed the city. Thus the armies of Ai were caught between two powerful branches of Joshua's army and had no choice but to fall by the sword. They were totally slaughtered; not one survived.

By any count, many thousands of troops were involved in the battle for Ai, and perhaps several thousand more stayed with Joshua to participate in the decoy maneuver. And each soldier, whether a front-line fighter or a noncombatant "decoy," was equally necessary for the victory.

Just as Joshua could not claim the promise of God for himself alone but needed the help of many others, so we cannot win against Satan on our own.

Distinguishing a Battle From a War

Every war is a series of battles. Dozens of battles may be won or lost without necessarily determining the outcome of the war. In the end it comes down to a question of strategy and patience. The winner is the one who comes out on top when the "bell rings."

As Christians we are aware that Satan does often appear to win some battles. After all, he tempts believers to sin, he contributes to the breakup of families, and he destroys the witness of many. To the watching world, and even to some Christians, it appears that he is on a winning streak. What could be clearer than the fact that evil is on the increase, the witness of the church is losing its appeal, and Satan is playing havoc with God's people? Yet for all that, we must remember that his victory is only a mirage; it is not real.

Joshua was not concerned about losing a battle as long as he knew that the war was being won. When he and his troops ran from Ai, a casual observer may have been tempted to think that Ai had the upper hand. But Joshua's loss was only a mirage; it was only temporary and actually served to hasten the defeat of the enemy.

God would fight for Joshua. This was simply another step in occupying the land that had already been deeded to Israel. No judgment should be made on the basis of the apparent disarray of Joshua's army. The outcome was never in doubt.

Let it be emphatically said that Satan will never have the satisfaction of winning even so much as one permanent victory. Not even the most insignificant battle is ever his. When he stops to savor the damage done on this planet, he need only remember that his final judgment is that much greater. Every victory eventually slips through his fingers, hastening his humiliation and torture. The higher he crawls, the farther he falls.

Satan is very intelligent, but he is not wise. Wisdom would dictate that he cease and desist any activity against God. Why enjoy the temporary glee of victory when your torment in eternal hell will only be that much greater?

Like Ai's troops coming out of the city, Satan is on the attack, fragmenting the Christian church and causing us to lose ground. But even while he is enjoying our plight, God is planning his demise. If we could see the big picture we would realize that God is moving His troops into position to increase Satan's humiliation.

King Pyrrhus defeated the Romans at Asculum in 279 B.C. But his victory came at tremendous personal cost. He is recorded as saying, in effect, "If I have another victory like this, I am going to be destroyed!" From his experience comes our phrase "Pyrrhic victory"—a victory that is too costly to the victor.

With the kind of victories Satan wins, he most certainly is headed for destruction. We can take heart even after a stinging defeat. The triumph of Christ is absolutely certain. Faced with this truth, Satan becomes completely impotent, forced to admit that his very next move is to his detriment. Even when he wins, he loses.

Don't judge the battle by how it is going today. Step back and catch a glimpse of how it is going to end. Satan and his legions are cast into the lake of fire and have all eternity to ponder the stupidity of their fights against God—an eternity of humiliation, shame, and torment.

When we are attacked by Satan his first goal is to bring us out from under the conscious protection of Christ and force us to focus on our circumstances. Daily he pounds against our bodies and minds, hoping to pry us loose from God's promises. He will use any technique to distract us from the resources we have in Christ.

The farther we run the less strength we have, until we are spiritually exhausted trying to fight Satan on largely our own initiative. Rather than fleeing to Christ, we dart off to all of the moving targets in our path. If we ever need to retreat, let it be to the Lord: "The name of the Lord is a strong tower; the righteous runs into it and is safe" (Prv 18:10).

God has given us powerful weapons so that we can detect and dislodge the enemy. Paul wrote, "For though we walk in the flesh, we do not war according to the flesh, for the weapons of our warfare are not of the flesh but divinely powerful for the destruction of fortresses" (2 Cor 10:3-4).

Suppose you lived in a walled city next to an enemy who regularly came over the north wall to plunder you and your family. Would you not make sure that particular part of the wall would be strengthened? Would not the city council set up guards to ward off the intruders and warn the inhabitants of a coming invasion?

How can we prevent being overrun by the enemy, so we can break the cycle of defeat? How can we reclaim territory that once was under our control but is now under the possession of Satan and his demons? The answer, as we shall see at the end of this chapter, is good strategy.

No Compromise With the Enemy

Compromise is often necessary in life. Differences sometimes call for thoughtful compromise. But compromise with Satan is always destructive. We can be flexible with our preferences, but we must be firm with our convictions.

We now come to a passage that has elicited much criticism from Bible scholars. Here we have an example of what many view as brutality on God's part. Joshua exterminated all the people of Ai, including women and children:

> Now it came about when Israel had finished killing all the inhabitants of Ai in the field in the wilderness where they pursued them, and all of them were fallen by the edge of the sword until they were destroyed, then all Israel returned to Ai and struck it with the edge of the sword. And all who fell that day, both men and women, were 12,000—all the people of Ai. For Joshua did not withdraw his hand with which he stretched out the

javelin until he had utterly destroyed all the inhabitants of Ai.

JOSHUA 8:24-26

Brutality! Cruelty! Women and children massacred along with the men of war, all done under the direction of Almighty God!

Several matters must be kept in mind. First, God was patient with the Canaanites, such as the people of Ai. Centuries earlier He told Abraham that his seed (the Israelites) would be in Egypt for four hundred years, because "the iniquity of the Amorite is not yet complete" (Gn 15:16). Now, as the Israelites returned under Joshua, these people had finally reached the point where they were irredeemably wicked.

Archeologists tell us that the Canaanites practiced every form of sexual perversion known to man. They sacrificed their children to pagan gods. Their culture was thoroughly saturated with evil.

Second, there was always the possibility that if some of the inhabitants had lived they would have eventually brought moral pollution to the Israelites. Israel tended to adopt the gods of their pagan neighbors.

Some liberal scholars say that the Bible is nothing more than a record of man's understanding of God. Therefore, the argument goes, we can see evolution in the Bible's conception of God. The God of the Old Testament is cruel and barbaric, whereas the God and Father of our Lord Jesus Christ is loving and kind.

But those of us who accept the whole Bible as a revelation from God believe that the character of God does not evolve, "For I, the Lord, do not change" (Mal 3:6).

In the Old Testament there were at least thirteen different sins, such as adultery and homosexuality, that demanded the death penalty. In the New Testament there is no such punishment prescribed for these sins. Has God changed His mind? Has He mellowed? Was He cruel in the Old Testament and compassionate in the New? The answer, of course, is that God has not changed. Nor has His opinion of these sins been revised. The character of God is the same from generation to generation.

The bottom line is that we have little choice but to accept God as He is, even when He appears ruthless and cruel. It does little good to protest, as some do, "My God would never approve of what Joshua did!"

It is not for us to remake God into an image that is better suited to our sensitive tastes. If He approved of the massacre described here, so be it. No wonder that we read in the New Testament, "It is a terrifying thing to fall into the hands of the Living God" (Heb 10:31).

I've asked you to let the battle of Ai represent our war with Satan. Just as Joshua would not compromise with his mortal enemy, we mustn't either. Of course we cannot exterminate Satan like Joshua did Ai, but we must realize that we are in a fight to the finish, we are in mortal combat, and the stakes are high.

Eventually Satan will be crushed, thrown into the lake of fire, forever tormented for his deeds. The outcome of the war is not in doubt. But between now and then there are many battles for each of us to fight.

Remember the Source of Blessing

When the battle at Ai was over, Joshua took the people thirty miles north to the valley between Mount Ebal and Mount Gerizim to celebrate the victory. Half of the tribes stood on Ebal (the mount of cursing), and the others stood on Mount Gerizim (the mount of blessing). While these many thousands stood, "He read all the words of the law, the blessing and the curse, according to all that is written in the book of the law. There was not a word of all that Moses had commanded which Joshua did not read before all the assembly of Israel with the women and the little ones and the strangers who were living among them" (Jos 8:34-35).

Historians are puzzled by Joshua's decision to lead hundreds of thousands of people to these mountains in the middle of the land at a time of war. Though he had already conquered Ai and Bethel, there were other undefeated Canaanite cities such as Shechem and Hazor. Taking the people through enemy territory certainly was a military risk.

Why did Joshua dare to stage this celebration amid a series of battles? He was absolutely convinced that the triumphs they had experienced would cause the people to forget that success was tied to obedience to God. He feared they would take victory for granted and become lax in their commitment to the Book of the Law. This, in the final analysis, is the only way to detect and defeat the enemy: consistent obedience to the Word of God.

There is a touch of irony in the victory at Ai: God told Joshua that the people were allowed to keep the spoil of the city. Unlike Jericho, the wealth of Ai was theirs. If only Achan had had the patience to wait for God's timing, he might have ended up with a beautiful garment and a fistful of money after all! Even what God wants us to have must be had in God's time.

Historians tell us that there was a naval battle in the sixteenth century between the forces of Venice and Genoa. The Genoese suffered a crushing defeat. But after the damage to their ships had been repaired, the commander asked his forces to return to fight the fleets of Venice one more time. His compatriots objected, wondering how they could be asked to return to fight an enemy who had beaten them so badly. But the commander replied, "It was rendered famous by our defeat; let us render it immortal by our victory."

God wants us to return to the place of our defeat. He wants to win great victories in the very areas of our lives that have been ravaged by Satan.

Let's not let our first bitter experience at Ai prevent us from a return journey. The second time the victory will be all the sweeter.

Chapter Ten

Living With a Bad Decision
(Read Joshua 9)

We've all made decisions we have regretted. One evening I made a snap decision to buy a sports coat. Even before I got home I knew I didn't like it. A few months later my wife and I packed several boxes of clothing to give away and I included that coat. To purchase it was foolish, but it had no lasting consequences. If only all bad decisions were that easy to dispense with!

If you buy an overpriced house and then find you can't make the payments, that is more serious. A friend of mine borrowed a substantial amount of money to buy some stock that was guaranteed to zoom upward; instead it zoomed downward and he had to sell his house to cover the loan.

Even these bad decisions are not as serious as marrying "the wrong one." A woman may marry a non-Christian and find that her values are in conflict; there may be serious problems of adjustment. Or perhaps both are Christians but the marriage is a mismatch. Six months after the wedding neither can figure out why they ever married.

Bad decisions are legion. Some are serious, others are not, but we have all made them. What do we do with them?

Even Joshua made a bad decision. He had a string of victories to his credit shortly after he marched into Canaan. Various tribes banded together to fight him but fell before his military expertise. Thanks to the faithfulness of God, he was on a roll.

One pagan town decided to come up with a creative strategy to save their lives. They chose to trick Joshua into believing that they had come from a far country and then proceeded to make a peace treaty with him. Evidently these shrewd people knew that God forbade the Israelites to make a treaty with the people of Canaan (see Ex 23:31-33). So if they could con Joshua into believing that they had come from another country, he might fall for the bait. Once the treaty was made they would be spared.

Satan does the same to us today. Sometimes he is like a roaring lion; at other times he is as subtle as a snake. As a last resort he offers us a peace treaty, hoping we will become entangled by a chain of our own making. He wants us to make a decision we will not be able to back out of.

Let's follow the strategy as it unfolds.

The Trap Is Laid

The inhabitants of Gibeon took worn sacks and old wineskins on their donkeys and put patched sandals on their feet. They put moldy bread in their satchels and wore threadbare clothing. All of this made it appear as if they had come from a great distance, when in fact they had just come from Gibeon, eight miles away.

When they came to Joshua they had their speech ready: "We have come from a far country; now therefore, make a covenant with us" (Jos 9:6). They deceived Joshua by lying about their origin. These deceivers remind us of Satan who does the same to us, pretending to be from God. There are some people who actually claim to hear inner voices that give them guidance. The source of these revelations must be carefully checked. Just because such voices may say good things or even quote Scripture does not prove that they originate from God. Recall that Satan quoted Scripture to Christ, attempting to deceive even the Son of God.

Many people have been cruelly misled by teachers, counselors, and even pastors who have claimed to speak for God but have given unwise counsel. The source of our information is very important, for deceptions abound.

The Gibeonites also lied about their intentions. They told Joshua that they wanted a covenant because they had heard about the wonders of the Lord God. They gave the impression that they longed to honor God.

We have all heard the old adage, "If you can't lick 'em, join 'em." When the enemy has the advantage he is not satisfied with anything less than total control and the eventual destruction of the people of God. But when he is cornered and must confess to the authority of the Lord's servants, he presses for compromise. He seeks a treaty of peace.

Perhaps the best example is when we compromise with sin, believing that we are able to control the extent of our involvement and contain the consequences. Eventually, we become ensnared with the sin with which we have made a covenant.

Whenever the nation Israel made a league with pagan nations, God judged His people by allowing them to be ensnared by the nation with whom the covenant was made.

The sin we toy with becomes the trap that wounds us.

The Bait Is Chosen

Notice the Gibeonites appealed to Joshua's pride. They came pretending to want to be his servants. They honored him, thus putting him in a position of vulnerability: "Your servants have come from a very far country because of the fame of the Lord your God; for we have heard the report of Him and all that He did in Egypt.... So our elders and all the inhabitants of our country spoke to us, saying, 'Take provisions in your hand for the journey, and go to meet them and say to them, "We are your servants; now then, make a covenant with us"'" (Jos 9:9, 11).

They humbly acknowledged that Joshua was the servant of the Most High God and, by implication, that they wanted to worship the true God also. They tried to get Joshua to see the advantages of ratifying a covenant with them. In effect they said, "We will make life easier for you by being your servants." They were using the strategy of Satan, who told Eve that if she took his suggestion, she would be "like God, knowing good and evil."

Satan always makes us think that his suggestions are for our good. "You owe it to yourself to become rich," he whispers to a businessman who is about to cheat to make a deal. Or, "You deserve this bit of pleasure," he says to the lonely single who is contemplating an illicit sexual relationship.

As the final act of humility, the strangers invited Joshua to inspect their bread and worn clothing. He could see and feel for himself the trustworthiness of their words.

The Trap Is Sprung

Joshua took the moldy bread in his own hands; he saw the old wineskins and the worn shoes. Then ominously we read, "So the men of Israel took some of their provisions, and did not ask for the counsel of the Lord. And Joshua made peace with them and made a covenant with them, to let them live; and the leaders of the congregation swore an oath to them" (Jos 9:14-15).

Why did Joshua fall into the trap of the enemy? For one thing, he acted on superficial evidence. Human observation cannot always give a proper diagnosis of a situation. What appeared to be obvious was actually complex. Something was hidden that escaped the attention of the human eye.

Seldom is a situation what it appears to be. Only God, who can see beyond the disguises, is qualified to give us guidance in the decisions of life.

A Christian couple investigated a particular area, hoping to buy a house. Finally, they saw one that appeared to meet their needs exactly—the right size, the right area, and the right amenities. But their loan application was held up, and they were unable to make good on the offer they had made. Before they could redeem the situation, the house was sold "from under their nose."

How disappointing! Yet six months later they learned that one of the walls of the basement in that house had collapsed! Think of how fortunate they were to have been spared the grief of fixing such a faulty structure.

When we interpret situations according to human observation, the possibility of error is great. Seldom is something what it appears to be. That's why we must seek God even in the details of life.

Second, Joshua neglected prayer. He "did not ask for the counsel of the Lord." Why did he not pray? It certainly was not because he was carnal or rebellious. Joshua walked with God, obeying to the best of his ability.

Joshua did not ask God because his decision looked so right, so obvious. Also, the matter seemed rather trivial— should we bother God about everything? The battles were now going well; there seemed no reason to have to rely on God for a decision that appeared rather routine.

How often we make mistakes because we do what appears to be wise or obvious to us. Or possibly we do not ask God's guidance because we are afraid that He might say no to something we desperately want to do. So a businessman makes his investment without prayer; a young woman chooses to marry her lover without giving God a chance to break up the relationship. In these and a thousand other instances, people have made their own decisions, only to live with regret and failure.

Three days later, Joshua found out that the Gibeonites lived only a few miles away. "And it came about at the end of three days after they had made a covenant with them, that they heard that they were neighbors and that they were living within their land" (v. 16).

He deeply regretted his vow of peace, but there was nothing he could do. In those days it was not fashionable to hire a team of lawyers to break an agreement. Rather, the person who was respected was the one who "swears to his own hurt, and does not change" (Ps 15:4). Joshua and the leaders had promised that the Gibeonites would live. They could not go back on their word.

How many people do you know who make a promise that they regret and keep it anyway? Think of the number of times we have broken our promises because it was inconvenient to keep them! Blessed is the one who swears to his own hurt and yet does not change the terms of the agreement.

Is it ever right to break a vow? Yes, if it is made to Satan, it should be broken immediately. The reason is because Satan has no right to any person, therefore any agreement with him is illegitimate. Suppose you came to me and announced that you had sold my children into slavery. Such an agreement would be invalid because you do not own my children. You can sell only what you own. God, not Satan, owns the people of the world.

A second instance where a vow can be broken is in the controversial matter of divorce. Though it was never God's intention to have a married couple separate, Moses did allow divorce "for the hardness of people's hearts." When Christ was pressed about whether it was right to divorce for any cause He said, "And I say to you, whoever divorces his wife, except for immorality, and marries another woman commits adultery" (Mt 19:9). Thus He specified the marriage covenant could be broken under the condition of immorality.

But God is not pleased with those who break their promises, especially if those promises are made as solemn vows. "When you make a vow to God, do not be late in paying it, for He takes no delight in fools. Pay what you vow! It is better that you should not vow than that you should vow and not pay" (Eccl 5:4-5).

To Joshua's everlasting credit, he did not go back on his word but honored the treaty. The Gibeonites were with him to stay.

Living With the Consequences

What were the consequences of this decision? The Gibeonites were cursed by Joshua, but God graciously chose to mix some blessing with the curse. The Almighty is never at a loss when confronted by human blunders. He *always* can take a difficult situation and turn it into a blessing. Every cloud has its silver lining, every thornbush its rose.

No doubt Joshua regretted many times that he had been tricked into making this treaty. The Gibeonites were a constant thorn in his side. Though God used them for blessing, this rash decision had its consequences.

How did God's grace work through a bad decision to bring about good?

1. The Gibeonites Aided in the Worship of God

"Now therefore, you are cursed, and you shall never cease being slaves, both hewers of wood and drawers of water for the house of my God" (Jos 9:23). The Gibeonites were condemned to be servants, but they would exercise their service in the temple of God! There they would see worship take place; there they would help the Israelites acknowledge the true and living God. Even the lowest kind of service done to aid in God's worship is blessed with dignity.

2. The Gibeonites Provided a Context for the Power of God

We're all acquainted with the story of how the sun stood still in response to Joshua's prayer (to be considered in the next chapter). What we sometimes forget is that the battle took place because Joshua was committed to defending the Gibeonites. The coalition of kings that Joshua fought were intent on attacking Gibeon for their covenant with Israel (see Jos 10:3-5).

The Israelites would never have seen the power of God in this battle had it not been for their forbidden treaty.

3. The Gibeonites Display the Grace of God

As the years progressed, the Gibeonites were given greater responsibilities. There is some evidence that during the time of Ezra they actually helped the Levites with their priestly responsibilities, for when Ezra lists those who returned with him from Babylon he includes 220 of the temple servants, whom David and the princes had given for the service of the Levites (see Ezr 8:20). Under Nehemiah, the Gibeonites are listed as helping in building the wall of Jerusalem close to what was known as the Old Gate: "Next to them Melatiah the Gibeonite and Jadon the Meronothite, the men of Gibeon and of Mizpah, also made repairs for the official seat of the governor of the province beyond the River" (Neh 3:7).

We should never underestimate God's ability to take a curse and turn it into a blessing. He can take grief and turn it into glory and put gladness into the grind.

Perhaps it is easier to live with wrong decisions we have made than to accept the destructive decisions of others who have wronged us. When someone has ruined our life it is difficult to see the silver lining on the edge of the dark cloud. Yet even here the finger of God can be seen.

The singer Ethel Waters was known to many through her recordings and especially her solos at Billy Graham Crusades. Ethel was born as the result of the rape of a fifteen-year-old girl. She grew up in poverty and without love. "Every child should have a knee to sit on," Ethel would say, "but I didn't have anyone who would hold me on their lap." Yet, for all the hurt, Ethel said that she spent so much time praising the Lord that she did not have time for self-pity. She is best known for singing:

> Why should I feel discouraged?
> Why should the shadows come?
> Why should my heart feel lonely?
> And long for heaven and home?
> When Jesus is my portion,
> My constant friend is He.
> His eye is on the sparrow,
> And I know He watches me;
> His eye is on the sparrow,
> And I know He watches me.

Does God have a plan for someone who, strictly speaking, should not have been born? Of course He does. Whether the bad decision is ours or that of someone else, God is well able to find a place for us within the wide circumference of His love and grace.

Joshua learned, as all of us must, that God is greater than our mistakes. Blessed are all those who can see stars in the darkest night.

Chapter Eleven

The Power of Prayer
(Read Joshua 10)

Think of the excitement of being in a war when God fights for you!

We've all been trampled by enemies, banged around by circumstances, and wearied with our obligations. How wonderful it would be if God would come to our rescue, take up our cause, and lead us to victory.

Joshua experienced a dramatic answer to prayer: The Lord performed a miracle to help him win a war. We read, "The Lord fought for Israel" (Jos 10:14). God was not only waiting in the wings in case Joshua needed help, but He directly intervened to help the Israelites win the battle.

God fights for us too. If He were not constantly taking our side in the conflicts of life, we would have been destroyed by Satan long ago. Sin would have already eroded every vestige of our character, and today we would be enslaved to passions that would eventually destroy us. God always fights for His people.

I'm convinced that when we get to heaven God will show us the full impact of our prayers. We will learn that God protected us and fought for us hundreds of times, even when we were unaware of it.

Joshua's story illustrates the great lengths to which God is willing to go to live up to His promises. When He says He is on our side, He means it. He will use His vast resources to make good on His Word.

The Gibeonites, you will recall, had tricked Israel into making a treaty with them. This meant, among other things, that they now came under the protection of Joshua and his army.

This new coalition was a threat to the other kings of the area. So the pagan king Adonizedek, who was the king of Jerusalem, recruited four other kings to wage war against the city of Gibeon: "Come up to me and help me, and let us attack Gibeon, for it has made peace with Joshua and with the sons of Israel" (v. 4).

Joshua was in a tight place; he had little choice but to defend the Gibeonites. They pleaded with him, "Do not abandon your servants; come up to us quickly and save us and help us, for all the kings of the Amorites that live in the hill country have assembled against us" (v. 6). They appealed to Joshua for help, and he responded by mobilizing his forces for battle.

The Lord gave Joshua the assurance that he was to take on these enemies and destroy them: "And the Lord said to Joshua, 'Do not fear them, for I have given them into your hands; not one of them shall stand before you'" (v. 8).

Previously, Joshua had conquered the land city by city, but now he had to face five foes at once. Because of his impressive record, they chose to gang up on him. His prior victories were a prelude to this greater conflict. Once again he was forced to trust in God.

Stop for a moment and let these kings represent your enemies. In previous chapters I have asked you to identify those barriers that keep you from spiritual growth and realistic optimism. What sin or weakness has you by the throat and is about to choke your spiritual life? By now I hope that you have come to name the kings that are plotting against you.

The moment we attack one of these "kings" we can expect others to come to his defense. Remember that the sins, habits, and attitudes that ensnare us are empowered by two forces working in tandem with each other. The first is the flesh, that sinful nature of ours that gives us the propensity to sin. These sins tend to work together in clusters, each strengthening the other. The second force is Satan and his demonic spirits, who magnify our sins so that they overwhelm us.

Whenever we make progress in one area of our lives, we are attacked in another. If we take a step to the right, we can expect an attack from the left. One step forward and we will be unexpectedly hit from the rear. These "kings" are well organized and will use any deception imaginable to win.

Yet God came to Joshua's aid, winning a big victory over a pagan coalition. Why was Joshua's prayer so effective?

He Prayed With a Promise

Notice the awesome words Joshua spoke in the sight of all Israel: "O sun, stand still at Gibeon, and O moon in the valley of Aijalon" (Jos 10:12). Let no one accuse him of making a trifling request!

Though we may think that his prayer was presumptuous, it was answered by God. We read, "So the sun stood still, and the moon stopped, until the nation avenged themselves of their enemies" (v. 13). Immediately he got the miracle he had asked for.

What gave Joshua the right to make such a large request and receive such a ready answer?

First, God had just restated the promise given to Joshua in the beginning of his leadership: "Do not fear them, for I have given them into your hands; not one of them shall stand before you" (v. 8). If we become weary with repetition, let us remember that we need to hear the words of God time and again if we wish to exercise power over the enemy. Too often we think of the promises of God as distant memories rather than present realities. The only way we can remedy that deficiency is to refresh our souls in what God has said.

Joshua took full advantage of the specific promise of God by mixing it with faith. The Book of Hebrews speaks of those who heard the Word of God but did not profit from it, "because it was not united by faith in those who heard" (Heb 4:2).

When Crowfoot, the great chief of an Indian tribe in southern Alberta, Canada, gave the Canadian Pacific Railroad permission to cross Indian territory, he was given a lifetime railroad pass on the CPR. He gratefully received it, put it in a leather case, and carried it around his neck for the rest of his life. There is no record, however, that he ever used his privilege.

We can be surrounded by the promises of God and yet be powerless. They can stay bound in leather, never used to enlist His power. Promises in themselves are like a check, of little value unless it is signed.

Joshua was so filled with faith that he actually spoke to the sun and moon, taking complete authority over them. Interestingly, Jesus said that if you have faith as a mustard seed, "you shall say to this mountain, 'Move from here to there,' and it shall move; and nothing shall be impossible to you" (Mt 17:20).

But even some Christians who speak so confidently about taking authority over the enemy may not see dramatic answers to prayer. Authority is never automatic; it comes through humility, submission, knowing the Word, and discipline.

Joshua could make such a great request because he knew that the value of a promise is dependent on the power and character of the one who gives it. If a person promises you a million dollars, it is important to find out whether he has the money to fulfill his word.

The "Member FDIC" sign we see in banks means that the account is backed by the resources of the federal government. But if the government is broke (as it often seems to be!) the guarantee is worthless. A question we must settle when we believe a promise is: Does the person have the resources to back up his words with deeds?

There is a second question we must ask about a promise-maker: Is he dependable? A person with a doubtful reputation may have a million dollars, but because he is dishonest his promise is worthless.

God has both the power and the integrity to meet all of His promised obligations. If He says that Joshua will win a battle, He will change the course of nature to make sure it will happen. Nothing can stand in the way of God's fulfilling His word.

God has the *power* to fulfill His promises: "For nothing will be impossible with God" (Lk 1:37). And He has the *integrity* to do so as well: "Thy word is truth" (Jn 17:17). God has the two attributes essential for making promises come true.

Joshua knew that God deserved to be believed.

He Prayed With Power

Joshua knew what it would take to win this battle. He saw that the forces of nature had to cooperate with him if he were to have the advantage. He spoke directly to the sun and moon, asking them to fight on his behalf.

There are several interpretations of what happened on that eventful day.

A popular view is that Joshua needed more time and so God actually gave him an extension of light. The sun and moon were slowed in their courses to give extra hours so he could win the battle.

Of course this immediately leads us into conflict with science. For the sun is already standing still; it is the earth that is in rotation. Strictly speaking the earth would have had to slow its pace to provide the extra time.

(By the way, I should point out that modern almanacs, just like the Bible, are written in the language of appearances. Weathermen speak of the sun "rising" and "setting." I've never heard anyone say, "The earth is rotating toward the sun at an angle and speed that will enable us to see the sun tomorrow at 7:45 A.M.")

Is it feasible to think that the earth might have slowed its rotation? Since the earth is traveling at about a thousand miles an hour at the equator, any change in speed would have created a massive catastrophe, short of further divine intervention.

A second possibility is that God did a local miracle that did not involve the rotation of the whole earth. In some inexplicable way, God gave Joshua more sunlight. Evidently, God caused such a miracle during the days of King Hezekiah when the shadow actually went backward on the sundial (see Is 38:8).

However, the phrase "the sun stood still" can also be interpreted to mean that the sun simply stopped its shining.

This third interpretation is more consistent with the battle strategy that was being played out in the valley. Joshua left Gilgal and marched all night, a distance of about twenty miles. It is unlikely that he needed more hours to fight, since he had the whole day ahead of him. What he needed was darkness for a cover and relief from the burning sun.

According to this interpretation, God dramatically answered his prayer by not only sending a cloud cover to blot out the rays of the sun, but with those clouds came a massive hailstorm that killed more of the enemy than Joshua's army did.

We read, "And it came about as they fled from before Israel, while they were at the descent of Beth-horon, that the Lord threw large stones from heaven on them as far as Azekah, and they died; there were more who died from the hailstones than those whom the sons of Israel killed with the sword" (Jos 10:11).

The cloud cover and hail boosted the morale of Joshua's army; Israel got shade and the pagans got hail. When God miraculously intervened, it threw the enemy into confusion. The coalition's strategy became unraveled, and they began to fall into disorder and fear.

Don't interpret this to mean that Joshua did nothing. He and his army had to continue to fight. When God fights for us He gives us the authority to overcome the enemy, but He does not do it independently of our own efforts.

God wins victories for us but not apart from us. We still must face our enemies, but we do not do it alone.

No wonder Joshua was able to exercise such awesome authority.

God could send a hailstorm, or He could change the rotation of the earth when and if this was necessary (as some interpretations assert). God will never allow His reputation to be tarnished. What He has promised He will perform.

Contrast this with Satan, who also makes a host of promises. Every one of his promises is based on a lie. His word lacks both integrity and power. Those who serve him the best end up the worst. Just ask Judas.

Joshua saw this battle in balance. He knew that the coalition of kings was much stronger than he. On the other hand he was not intimidated by them, since God was on his side. He knew that God would go to great lengths to fulfill His promises.

He Prayed With Participation

Here again we see the cooperation of human effort and God's power. One might think that when God fought there would be nothing for Joshua to do—just "let go and let God." But the promises of God do not exempt us from a battle; they just give us the ability to win it. Though God fights for us, He does not fight without us. He is a General who leads us into battle; we do not have the luxury of staying at home waiting for second-hand reports of how the war is progressing.

After Joshua exterminated their armies, the five kings ran to hide in the cave of Makkedah. Joshua might have said that the battle was over, so everyone could go home. But he was not satisfied. Even after a battle is over there are mopping up operations that must be completed.

The first step was to roll large stones against the mouth of the cave, thereby guarding the entrance so that the kings would not escape. While a few men did this, others of the Israelite army continued to kill the fleeing members of the pagan armies.

Then Joshua said, "Open the mouth of the cave and bring these five kings out to me from the cave" (Jos 10:22). These kings then had their necks broken, and they were hung on five separate trees all night. Everyone knew that the victory was complete.

Joshua knew that you can neither ignore nor compromise God's instructions. If God said that the inhabitants of the land had to be exterminated, Joshua was ready to obey.

Our battles with the flesh and the devil are never over in this life. We do not have the privilege of exterminating our enemy as Joshua did. Just when we think we have won over our enemy, another foe takes his place. Win as many battles as you like and you still cannot afford to take your armor off. Tomorrow is a new day with a new surprise and an unexpected enemy. And yesterday's victory is of no help.

But what a day Joshua had! We read, "And there was no day like that before it or after it, when the Lord listened to the voice of a man; for the Lord fought for Israel" (v. 14). Joshua proves that when we know the promises of God and are convinced of the power of God, we can exercise the authority of God. *We have as many promises as we need to do the will of God.*

Donald Grey Barnhouse tells the story of the wife of a French pastor who had made a "promise box" by hand, writing perhaps two hundred promises in French. Through the years her family used this box, and they were taught to trust in the Lord.

But during the war they fell into hard times. No food was

available except messes of potato peelings from a restaurant. Her children were emaciated; they cried to her for food. In one of her most tragic moments she turned to the promise box in desperation. She prayed, "Lord, I have such a great need. Is there a promise that is really for me? Show me, O Lord, what promise I can have in time of nakedness, peril, and sword."

She was blinded by her tears, and as she reached out for the box, she knocked it over. The promises showered down around her, on her lap and on the floor. She realized in a moment of supreme joy that all of the promises were indeed for her in the very hour of her greatest need. She learned that nothing can separate us from Christ's love—the promises were there to bless and encourage.

God is available for us today.

Chapter Twelve

Overcoming Obstacles
(Read Joshua 14)

"You can tell the character of a man by what it takes to stop him."

Of course that statement needs some qualifications, for we need to make sure that a person's goals are worthy before we talk about the toughness of character that keeps him going, no matter what. But some good men could have been great men if they had not stopped so soon.

Though we often see cowardice in the lives of others, it is not so easily detected in ourselves. I read that one day Soviet Premier Khrushchev was speaking before the Supreme Soviet and was severely critical of the late Joseph Stalin. During the speech someone sent up a note, "What were you doing when Stalin committed all those atrocities?"

"Who sent up this note?" Khrushchev shouted.

Not a person stirred.

"I'll give him one minute to stand up!"

Still no one stirred as the seconds ticked off.

"All right, I'll tell you what I was doing," Khrushchev began. "I was doing what the writer of this note was doing—*nothing!* I was afraid to be counted!"

Caleb was a man who was willing to be counted. He could

not be stopped. He had a dozen reasons why he could have chosen an early retirement. But at the age of eighty-five he kept taking territory for God.

Caleb had been one of the twelve spies sent ahead to check out the land of Canaan when Israel first arrived there forty years previously. You'll recall that ten of the men were frightened by the giants, the fortified cities, and the military expertise of the Canaanites. Only Caleb and Joshua encouraged the people to march ahead in the name of the Lord.

I'm told that the Chinese word for crisis is comprised of two characters, *way* and *gee*. Each of these is a word, the first meaning *danger* and the second meaning *opportunity*. Hence a crisis is quite literally a "dangerous opportunity."

When Moses sent the spies into the land, ten of them saw only the danger, two saw the opportunity. They knew that the greatest opportunity is sometimes fraught with the greatest danger.

Do you recall the name of even one of the other ten spies? If you do, I salute you! Very seldom do we remember the names of those who blend in with the majority. Most of our heroes are people who stood against the popular notions of their day and chose to forge ahead no matter what others thought. That's why we remember Caleb and Joshua.

God promised Caleb that he would conquer a piece of land for himself and his family once Joshua had crossed the Jordan (see Nm 14:24). Caleb now decided that he wanted the hill country of Hebron for his inheritance.

Just as Caleb chose his "mountain," so I encourage you to choose a mountain that you would like God to give you. Let that mountain be a spiritual challenge that has biblical support.

There is no promise in the Bible that God will allow you to become a millionaire before the age of fifty, or that you will eventually marry, or that you will be healthy all of your life. As mentioned in chapter 2, one reason there are so many people who are angry with God is because they trusted Him for blessings that are not specifically promised. Of course God often gives us these requests, but we must not presume; we can hold Him to only those promises that pertain to all believers.

Choose a mountain that is part of your inheritance as a Christian, such as victory over addictions, forgiveness that removes guilt, or the ability to withstand pressures at home or at work. These are the mountains we know God wants to conquer for us.

Let's consider some of the obstacles Caleb overcame to take his mountain for God.

His Friends

Surprisingly, friends often stand in the way of our spiritual progress. They give us bad advice; they discourage us by their words; and they encourage us to lead undisciplined lives. Or perhaps they feed our natural propensity to unbelief.

Think back to Caleb's experience. He was not only outvoted by his ten peers, but he was ridiculed by the multitude. He and Joshua stood alone in speaking out for God's faithfulness.

What did they get for their courage and faith? "But all the congregation said to stone them with stones" (Nm 14:10). The people would have killed them were it not for Moses' intervention.

If you are serious about taking some giant steps for God, realize that you might have to be misunderstood by your friends. In many subtle ways they may stand in the way of your spiritual development.

Recently I heard of a woman who chose to divorce her husband based on the counsel of her so-called Christian friends. Her only reason was that she was tired of the marriage, felt neglected, and thought she needed the freedom to "find herself." Friends who should be encouraging us to turn to God in our need sometimes turn us against Him.

If you have chosen to pursue God with all your heart, expect precious little support from others. Some will stand with you, but as Caleb learned, the ratio is about two to ten!

A friend of mine says he has learned to expect little from others but much from himself. That may sound cynical, but if interpreted in the right spirit, that philosophy might keep us from disappointment and give us the freedom to pursue God with or without the support of others.

There were other barriers Caleb had to cross to see his desire fulfilled.

Time

A total of forty years elapsed from the day God gave Caleb the promise until he was able to take his mountain for God. Thirty-eight of those years were spent wandering in the desert, and two more years had elapsed since Joshua started his military campaigns. Forty years is a long time.

Think of what Caleb had seen during that period of waiting!

He watched a whole generation die in the desert. His parents died; his friends died; and even the ten other spies died. Those were not easy years, for Caleb suffered along with the whole nation.

Caleb was there when the sons of Korah led a rebellion and God judged them; he saw the earth open up and swallow the rebels alive. Then additional thousands died in a plague when they grumbled at Moses and God for bringing them into the wilderness (see Nm 16).

Caleb suffered through all this because his fate was tied to that of the nation. If he thought he was wasting time in the desert, so be it; he had to wait it out. Though he was not personally disciplined by God, he was suffering because other people were under discipline. For all this, Caleb did not give up. Forty years later, he proved that God's promises were trustworthy.

How long have you waited for God to fulfill His Word? We can become impatient after six months or a year. Forty years seems incomprehensible. Yet sometimes God waits that long to do what we think He should do now.

Time is another barrier that must be overcome if we want to see God conquer that mountain. Patience (or perseverance) is one of the character traits God wants to develop in us (see Rom 5:3-4). There is only one way that patience can be nurtured, and that is by forcing us to wait for God's timing. Waiting for God is not a waste of time.

But Caleb had other forces working against him as he pursued his promise.

Racial Prejudice

You may be surprised to learn that Caleb was of mixed blood. He was the son of Jephunneh the Kenizzite (see Jos 14:6). This tribe belonged to the Canaanites, the very people who were to be exterminated! We first hear of them when God promised Abraham that his posterity would come out of Egypt and conquer Canaan. One of the wicked tribes that was to be harshly judged was the Kenizzites (see Gn 15:19).

Clearly, Caleb's family was originally outside of the covenant of blessing. Only a generous gift of God's grace kept him from being among the cursed. Evidently, some member of his family had gone down to Egypt with Abraham and therefore became a part of the "mixed multitude" Moses led out of Egypt with the children of Israel (see Ex 12:38). So Caleb participated in the blessing of God though his ancestors were outside of the sphere of God's chosen people.

I can't prove it from Scripture, but Caleb probably was ridiculed because he had Canaanite blood in his veins. The Jews habitually looked down on those who were of a mixed race and begrudged the grace of God to those who were deemed "impure." None of this, of course, would deter Caleb from following the Lord fully, for his focus was on God and not on the people who should have been supporting his faith. What a difference his perspective made!

Racial prejudice dies hard; perhaps it never really dies at all. There is something deeply demeaning about judging people on the basis of their ethnic background or skin color. Those who are shunned because of traits they were born with know how crippling such rejection can be.

Caleb, along with many others who have had to cope with such prejudice, have discovered that God is greater than the superficial judgments of thoughtless people. When God gives us a promise, nothing, except our own misplaced fear, can stop us from the blessing that accompanies it.

His Age

At eighty-five Caleb should have been asking for slippers instead of cleats! Who wants to go to war at this age, when there are so many able-bodied young men who can do it? He should have settled down in a condominium and hired a lawn service!

But Caleb was not content to relax when there was a promise to be fulfilled. God had told him that he would not only enter the Promised Land but also be personally involved in claiming territory for himself and his descendants. In fact, God kept him physically healthy with good eyesight so that he could see God's Word fulfilled: "I am still as strong today as I was in the day Moses sent me; as my strength was then, so my strength is now, for war and for going out and coming in. Now then, give me this hill country about which the Lord spoke on that day, for you heard on that day that Anakim were there, with great fortified cities; perhaps the Lord will be with me, and I shall drive them out as the Lord has spoken" (Jos 14:11-12).

Age is no barrier in doing the will of God. God keeps His people alive as long as they need to be in order to fulfill all that He has planned for them. There is no combination of men and demons, no illness or accident, that can end our lives before

God says that we have finished the work He has given us to do.

Most of the time when we speak about planning for retirement, we think of setting money aside so that we can have an enjoyable, stress-free environment in our final years. Perhaps what we should be thinking about is how we can use those last years for our most productive service for God. With a lifetime of experiences in proving the faithfulness of God, we should be well equipped in old age to claim our greatest mountains for God.

If you ask what those mountains might be, I can only say that God will guide us to those challenges if we honestly seek Him. Our greatest danger will be to shy away from consulting God lest He should upset our own self-made plans for our final years on earth.

There was one other obstacle Caleb had to overcome.

The Enemy

The Anakim had entrenched themselves on top of the hill of Hebron, the parcel of ground Caleb had chosen to conquer. They were living in a city with high walls; they were not about to give up easily their territory to Caleb and his troops.

Just because God had given Caleb a promise did not mean that he could relax and watch it happen. Yes, God was faithful, but Caleb had to have the courage to fight. To hold fast to the promises of God is not easy, but it is rewarding.

What made Caleb so different from the others around him? If we could talk with him I think he would say, "There is no obstacle too great for the promises of God."

From where did he get this faith that enabled him to believe God regardless of the discouragement of forty years of waiting? Obviously, if Caleb had focused on the obstacles, he never would have had the tenacity to capture a mountain for God. He learned the same lesson as Joshua: *Only those who gaze at the promises and glance at the problems move ahead against opposition.*

For we become what we gaze at—what we dwell on. The more we are absorbed by problems, the more formidable they become. The more we look at God's promises, the smaller the problems become. In fact, we can say that the size of our obstacles is really dependent on the size of our God. Big obstacles imply a small God; a big God implies that all obstacles are small.

William Carey was born in 1761 near Northampton, England. His childhood was routine, though he had persistent problems with allergies. He was a shoemaker from age sixteen to twenty-eight. He spent his free time in Bible study and learning about missions.

At the age of twenty he married Dorothy, an unfortunate mismatch from the beginning. Not only was she uneducated, as were most women in England at the time, but more seriously, she was totally disinterested in her husband's passion for the souls of India.

Their early years were filled with hardship and poverty. He accepted a call to become the pastor of a small Baptist church, where he was able to continue his studies. He became convinced that the Great Commission was central to the responsibility of the church. Though such an idea is not new to us, it was so revolutionary in his day that when he presented his vision to a group of ministers he was told, "Young man, sit down. When God pleases to convert the heathen, He will do it without your aid or mine."

But William Carey was undeterred in his zeal and helped organize a new mission board that eventually sent him to India. His church opposed his decision, and his father called him "mad." Worse, his wife adamantly opposed leaving her homeland to embark on a hazardous five-month voyage and spend the rest of her life in the deadly tropical climate of India. They had three children, with another on the way, and she was unwilling to go.

Incredibly, Carey was determined to leave, even if it meant going without her. He and John Thomas, a fellow missionary appointee, along with Carey's eight-year-old son, set sail for India. But the ship had to turn back at Portsmouth, England, for technical reasons, and Carey was forced to return home. Later, Dorothy, having now given birth to their fourth child, reluctantly agreed to go with him, provided that her sister accompany them.

Once in India the family faced a series of hardships. There was incredible poverty; just being able to eke out a living was difficult. Worse, Dorothy lost her health and mental stability. When their little five-year-old son Peter died, it escalated her mental deterioration. Coworkers described her as "wholly deranged."

Nevertheless Carey pressed ahead with his work. He spent hours each day in translation, preached, established schools, and eventually founded a church. Yet, at the end of seven years, Carey could not claim even one Indian convert. Later his help was needed in Serampore and he moved there.

While at Serampore, Carey completed three translations of the whole Bible and helped with translating sections of Scripture into several more languages and dialects. Though his translations were rough and often incomprehensible, he did not give up. He would rework a translation until he was convinced it could be understood. Along with these projects he founded a college and began churches. John Marshman wrote how Carey often worked on his translations, "while an insane wife, frequently wrought up to a state of most distressing excitement was in the next room."

Six months after Dorothy died in 1807, Carey remarried against the opposition of fellow missionaries. His second marriage, thankfully, was happy, and Carey's children at last had a mother who gave them her care and interest.

One of his most devastating setbacks was the loss of his priceless manuscripts in a fire in 1812. Destroyed were translations of the Bible, a huge multilingual dictionary, and grammar books. Think of it! Years of painstaking labor gone! A lesser man might never have recovered, but Carey took the fire as a judgment from God and began the arduous task all over again!

Carey spent his last years in dogged language study punctuated by internal disputes within the mission compound. New missionaries wanted improved living conditions and complained that the mission leadership was too dictatorial. Eventually a split ensued and a second mission board was formed. What made Carey's pain worse was that the mission board back in England chose to side with Carey's opponents.

Carey died in 1834, having had an impact on missions far beyond the land of India. He inspired thousands to take the

Great Commission seriously and give themselves to Bible translation and the establishment of churches (for further details, read Ruth Tucker's *From Jerusalem to Irian Jaya* [Grand Rapids, Mich.: Academie Books, 1983]).

Though William Carey may not have been such a good role model as a father, he can be a model to all of us in his single-minded determination to do what he believed God wanted. Why could he not be stopped? Carey had this to say about his success: "I can plod. I can persevere in any definite pursuit. To this I owe everything."

The spirit of William Carey, and of Caleb, can still be found in the church today. We all have known people who will overcome any obstacle to do what they believe to be the will of God.

When you have a promise from God, nothing need stop you from experiencing its fulfillment.

Chapter Thirteen

Making the Promises Work
(Read Joshua 21)

The greatest spiritual challenge we will ever face is to match the promises of God with our performance. No one should doubt that God is on our side; the question is: How can we enlist His power so as to see His promises come to pass?

If we think the Lord has failed us, we will be hesitant to cast ourselves on His Word. That's why our first attempts at serious faith are often halting, fraught with uncertainty.

Throughout these pages I have emphasized that the promises are not ours without a struggle. We often wrongly assume that they will automatically be fulfilled. This sets us up for a big disappointment, because we conclude that God is not as reliable as we are told He is.

The purpose of this chapter is to summarize the principles needed to apply the promises to the rough-and-tumble world of our experience. I hope to dispel the notion that God's promises can be enjoyed without effort and without sacrifice. But I also want to strongly affirm that God's promises, once unleashed, are everything they are made out to be.

Read this remarkable statement regarding the faithfulness of God: "So the Lord gave Israel all the land which He had sworn to give to their fathers, and they possessed it and lived in it. And the Lord gave them rest on every side, according to all that He had sworn to their fathers, and no one of all their enemies stood before them; the Lord gave all their enemies into their hand. *Not one of the good promises which the Lord had made to the house of Israel failed; all came to pass*" (Jos 21:43-45, italics mine).

Every word fulfilled!

What promises is the writer referring to? The basic one is, "Every place on which the sole of your foot treads, I have given it to you, just as I spoke to Moses. From the wilderness and this Lebanon, even as far as the great river, the river Euphrates, all the land of the Hittites, and as far as the Great Sea toward the setting of the sun, will be your territory. No man will be able to stand before you all the days of your life. Just as I have been with Moses, I will be with you; I will not fail you or forsake you" (Jos 1:3-5).

How do we move from point A to point B? That is, how do we get from the promise to its fulfillment? Joshua 1 is the promise, the next twenty-three chapters are the fulfillment, but what lies in between? There are six price tags that had to be paid to see it all happen. Without these, the promise would not have been fulfilled.

Conflict

This, of course, is the most obvious price that had to be paid for inheriting the land. Most of the Book of Joshua is a record of war. In the opening chapters the nation prepares for battle; in chapter 6 they capture Jericho; in chapter 8 they conquer

Ai, but not before they had lost thirty-six men on the battle-field. In subsequent chapters they engage in one military campaign after another. Why all these battles?

Some battles were internal because people could not get along with each other, or there was sin in the camp. There had to be internal unity before Joshua could continue his military conquests.

Most battles were external, against the Canaanites. Some of these were won more easily than others, but eventually Joshua took all the territory he wanted. Whenever he challenged the enemy in faith, he won.

Why is fighting necessary when taking territory for God? Remember that every step we take forward forces the enemy to take a step backward. This he is loath to do. Satan opposes every inch of our progress as Christians. As we advance, he must retreat, and this makes him angry. *There is no such thing as unopposed spiritual progress.*

Paul wrote, "For our struggle is not against flesh and blood, but against the rulers, against the powers, against the world forces of this darkness, against the spiritual forces of wickedness in the heavenly places" (Eph 6:12). We can be armed with all of God's promises and still have to do battle within our souls. Victory is never automatic. Only those who have the courage to "fight the good fight of faith" experience it.

The promises of God may lead to rest, but getting there involves conflict. We are not guaranteed success, only the assurance that we can conquer if we are persistent. God was faithful, but think of all the hassles Israel endured in seeing that faithfulness displayed!

Patience

Since we can read the Book of Joshua in an hour or two, it might be easy for us to think that Joshua conquered the land quickly, in a few days or weeks. Not so. The events of this book took about fourteen or fifteen years in all. At one point the Lord said to Joshua, "You are old and advanced in years, and very much of the land remains to be possessed" (Jos 13:1). Even when Joshua died there were still battles to be won, for there were pockets of resistance throughout the land. Yes, Joshua won many victories, but none was so decisive that it ended all the hostility of the enemy. In fact we read, "And the Lord your God will clear away these nations before you little by little; you will not be able to put an end to them quickly, lest the wild beasts grow too numerous for you" (Dt 7:22).

God's promises are not always fulfilled instantly. He would drive out the enemy a step at a time. The nation would win one victory, then regroup and go on to another. Year after year the battles continued with unrelenting resistance from the angry inhabitants. Indeed, the Lord said that the nation would not be able to handle complete victory if He gave it to them at once, for the wild beasts would multiply on territory that was conquered but not occupied.

Jesus said, "When the unclean spirit goes out of a man, it passes through waterless places seeking rest, and not finding any, it says, 'I will return to my house from which I came.' And when it comes, it finds it swept and put in order. Then it goes and takes along seven other spirits more evil than itself, and they go in and live there; and the last state of that man becomes worse than the first" (Lk 11:24-26). His point is that an empty life is open to all kinds of sinful influences. It is not enough to simply cast out the demons; the power of God must fill the void that remains. Unoccupied territory can be just as dangerous as territory inhabited by the enemy.

Joshua had to make sure that the land he conquered was properly occupied. The Israelites set up camps in it so that it would not be retaken.

The nation learned as it went along. Joshua would discuss strategy and design game plans as they moved along. Every new battle was a challenge of ingenuity and courage.

How wonderful it would be if we could have one spiritual experience whereby we could win all our battles at once! How discouraging it can be to have to fight every day. We are always looking for the big breakthrough, the one event that will catapult us to spiritual greatness.

I believe that we often do have crisis spiritual experiences that cause us to surge ahead in our fellowship with God. Sometimes it happens when we are backed into a corner and are forced to yield fully to the Lord. Or perhaps it comes at a special moment of fellowship with the Almighty. We are thankful for such times, but even then, the battles do not end.

Most of the time we win against the enemy by a series of lesser battles, those daily disciplines whereby we learn to say no to temptation and to live our lives for God.

So the question is not so much, Where are you in your Christian life? but rather, In what direction are you going? As you look back throughout the months and years, can you discern progress? Are you fighting the same old battles, or have you left them behind for new challenges?

Cooperation

Throughout the Book of Joshua we find the phrase, "The sons of Israel." It's a reference to the nation, of course, as it won battles, planned strategy, and celebrated its victories. Not even Joshua could take on the Canaanites by himself. Battles are won or lost by troops, tribes, or nations. The church that is strong will tend to strengthen its individual members; the weak church may sink those who are learning to swim.

Individualism makes us think we can live the Christian life alone. We think that because we have the promises of God, we can win private victories over our private (or not so private) defeats. Yet in Colossians Paul expresses the importance of our growing *together:* "That their hearts may be encouraged, having been knit together in love, and attaining to all the wealth that comes from the full assurance of understanding, resulting in a true knowledge of God's mystery, that is, Christ Himself" (Col 2:2). We can attain to our spiritual wealth only when our hearts are knit together in love. The promises of God must not be applied in isolation but within the context of the community of God's people.

Recently I spoke to a man who told me something he had never shared before. Though he had witnessed to nonbelievers in shopping malls and had even discipled several young Christians, he said, "I spend three to four hundred dollars a month on pornography."

I shared much with him about spiritual victory, but I quickly added, "You will never get out of this spiritual bondage alone." Not even Joshua was capable of taking on Jericho by himself! Personal accountability is essential in overcoming addictions, abuses, and other spiritual battles. Pray that God would give you a prayer partner with whom you can share your joys and sorrows. That is the first step in drawing strength from the body.

The promises of God are given within the context of the people of God; they are to be exercised within the believing community. There is a direct relationship between our strength and the combined strength of the entire church.

Submission

Once the major cities of Canaan were conquered, the land was divided among the various tribes of Israel. The apportionment was done by lot, or we would say by the throw of dice. This made all the decisions free of personal interest. Joshua could not be accused of favoritism or "stacking the deck."

In fact, this ancient practice had the blessing of God. "The lot is cast into the lap, but its every decision is from the Lord" (Prv 16:33). We could paraphrase it, "The dice are thrown upon the table, but the way they land is determined by God." This doesn't mean that we should live our lives by the roll of dice, for God has not promised to lead us that way today. But in Old Testament times He did use the lot to enable the people to make difficult decisions.

Predictably, some people were not happy with their lot. For example the sons of Joseph complained that their territory was too narrow: "Why have you given me only one lot and one portion for an inheritance, since I am a numerous people whom the Lord has thus far blessed?" (Jos 17:14).

Joshua tells them that they should conquer more territory for themselves. But they in turn complained about the size of the Canaanites in the land. Joshua countered with the challenge that they should not be intimidated by the enemy: "You are a numerous people and have great power; you shall not have one lot only, but the hill country shall be yours.... For you shall drive out the Canaanites, even though they have chariots of iron and though they are strong" (vv. 17-18).

This was Joshua's way of saying, "When life hands you a lemon, make lemonade!" They were to make the best of their "lot" whether they liked it or not. After all, it is God who determines the outcome. Yes, some people would be living closer to Jerusalem than others; some would have better pasture land or better grain fields. But no matter where God had placed them He would enlarge their territory right there.

Are you satisfied with your lot in life? We did not choose our parents, our appearance, or the level of our intelligence. We did not choose to be mistreated, to suffer from physical or spiritual affliction. These things are our lot, the "cards we were dealt," humanly speaking.

Through foolish choices and sins some people make their lot worse; some ruin their lives on the altar of bitterness or sensuality. They look across the fence and are consumed with jealousy because the people next door have a better lot in life.

How can the promises of God be applied right where we are? We must have the faith to believe that God is great enough to enable us to make the best of our lives despite the present situation we are in. As we shall see later, God is our lot, our portion. We can enjoy Him even if we are squeezed into a small parcel of land; that is, even if we must live our lives with a multitude of unfulfilled dreams.

The promises of God can be applied regardless of our lot. Our task is submission to God wherever He has placed us. As the adage says, "Bloom where you are planted!"

Faithful Obedience

So much has already been said about faith that I need only mention it here briefly. God repeatedly told Joshua that if he hoped to conquer the land he would have to obey in faith. The Israelites had two recurring fears during their conquest of Canaan: fear of their enemies and fear of being abandoned by God. Again and again they thought God would forsake them in their hour of need.

If we wonder how our faith can be increased, the answer is *through the Word of God.* "So faith comes from hearing, and hearing by the Word of Christ" (Rom 10:17). God's Word must constantly be pouring through our minds for cleansing and for increasing our faith. Without firm belief in the trustworthiness of God, we cannot move forward.

Watchfulness

The Israelites never did exterminate the Canaanites. Several times we read, "But they did not drive them out completely" (Jos 17:13). God used the remaining Canaanites to accomplish His purpose in the lives of His people. They were a constant reminder of their need for trust in the Lord, a constant warning against backsliding.

You and I will trust in ourselves for as long as we are able. By nature we turn to God only when we have a problem too great to handle. Nothing forces us to trust in God like confronting an enemy several times our size.

God also used the Canaanites to discipline Israel for disobedience. When the nation sinned, the Canaanites became strong enough to bring Israel to its knees. As the Book of Judges opens we have a long list of all the territories that were now under Canaanite control (see Jgs 1:3-36). The entire book recounts the cycles of discipline as God used the Canaanites to bring Israel to repentance.

There is an important principle found often in the Old Testament and implied in the New: *God always allows us to be ensnared by the enemy we make peace with.* The moment we tolerate some known sin, we find that we will eventually be overcome by it. Any agreements we reach between ourselves and the world are to our detriment. Neither Satan nor our sinful nature plays by the rules; the moment agreement is reached, the evil begins to take over.

I have emphasized that we are to conquer territory for the glory of God; but what is the territory we are to conquer? Using the analogy of physical territory, David spoke about the spiritual territory we should receive from God. He even spoke of this as his "lot," as the portion God had assigned to him:

The Lord is the portion of my inheritance and my cup; Thou dost support my lot. The lines have fallen to me in pleasant places; indeed, my heritage is beautiful to me. I will bless the Lord who has counseled me; indeed, my mind instructs me in the night. I have set the Lord continually before me; because He is at my right hand, I will not be shaken. Therefore my heart is glad, and my glory rejoices; my flesh also will dwell securely.

PSALM 16:5-9

David's inheritance is our inheritance today: To pursue the pleasures of God which can be ours through applying the promises of God. This will never be easy, but through faith it can be done. Little wonder Joshua was admonished that the Book of the Law should not depart out of his mouth, for it is only as we are absorbed in the Word that we can have the faith to stand on the promises, no matter what.

Chapter Fourteen

Choosing God
(Read Joshua 22–24)

We will never be able to shed the Grasshopper Complex unless we make some tough choices. Unfortunately, making a right decision is always more difficult than making a wrong one. Someone has accurately observed that the path of least resistance is what makes people and rivers crooked.

None of us can stay uncommitted indefinitely. We will either grow in our love for Christ or fall back into the desert with its boredom, aimlessness, and false promises of refreshment. Either we will take territory for God or we will hand it over to the enemy.

God will see to it that we are pushed off the fence, and sometimes none too gently! Time moves on; decisions must be made. God backs us into a corner, and we must make up our minds about ultimate priorities.

Our major life choices are based on a trail of lesser decisions we make from day to day. The direction of our lives is determined by our daily habits, our secret priorities.

Before he died Joshua poured out his heart to the Israelites, pleading with them to serve the Lord. He warned of the danger of compromise; he spoke of the judgment that would come for disobedience. And he offered hope and blessing to those who were prepared to follow the Lord fully.

But before Joshua issued his final challenge, he had to settle a dispute that had arisen among the tribes. There was the possibility of civil war, all because of a misunderstanding. Recall that the tribes of Reuben, Gad, and one-half the tribe of Manasseh had requested the opportunity of settling on the east side of the Jordan River. Joshua promised that they could claim this territory, but only after they had helped the other tribes conquer the land from the Canaanites (see Jos 1:12-18).

Now that these tribes had fulfilled their obligations, it was time for them to return to their allotments east of the Jordan. Joshua released them with his special blessing and an exhortation to faithfulness (see 22:5). As they left for home they remembered the faithfulness of God and their united struggle with all of the other tribes. To commemorate their friendship and common bond with those who would be on the western side of the Jordan, these tribes built an altar in honor of the Lord God.

However, this symbol of unity was misinterpreted by the other Israelites as a step toward apostasy. They gathered at Shiloh and prepared to go to war against the armies of the eastern tribes. Here was an altar, they thought, that would be used to worship pagan deities.

They appointed Phinehas, known for his righteous zeal, to lead a delegation to confront these tribes with the horror of what they were doing. The accusation was direct: "What is this unfaithful act which you have committed against the God of Israel, turning away from following the Lord this day, by building yourselves an altar, to rebel against the Lord this day?" (v. 16)

Fortunately, it was all a misunderstanding. The two-and-a-half tribes replied that they were not setting up an altar for rival worship but only as a memorial to the faithfulness of God: "If it was in rebellion, or if in an unfaithful act against the Lord do not Thou save us this day!" (v. 22). So began a long speech explaining the motivation behind this project. This altar, they explained, would be for a witness between the tribes that they are all to perform the service of the Lord. It would remind the Trans-Jordan tribes that they had a right to worship at Shiloh, where the one legitimate altar had been built.

Let's admire the spiritual zeal of the western tribes who, though weary of war, were ready to fight again for the purity of the worship of Jehovah. They knew full well the dangers of spiritual compromise; they understood that idolatry arises easily in the heart of mankind. They had to learn, however, that it is dangerous to prejudge the motives of others. Fortunately, this matter was properly resolved through confrontation and mutual understanding.

With that dispute settled, Joshua asked the nation of Israel to make a tough decision. He gave two farewell speeches. The first was apparently given at Shiloh, where he warned the people against any compromise with the nations of the land. They were to remember that God had been faithful in fighting all their battles: "For the Lord has driven out great and strong nations from before you; and as for you, no man has stood before you to this day. One of your men puts to flight a thousand, for the Lord your God is He who fights for you, just as He promised you" (23:9-10).

And what would happen if the people did forsake the Lord? These nations would grow strong, said Joshua, and would "be a snare and a trap to you, and a whip on your sides and thorns in your eyes, until you perish from off this good land which the Lord your God has given you" (v. 13).

The Israelites would have to learn a basic principle of God's discipline: *We become ensnared by the sin we tolerate.*

With this warning ringing in their ears, the nation gathered at Shechem to hear Joshua's final speech. Shechem is where Abraham first received the promise that his seed would inherit the land of Canaan; Jacob stopped at Shechem when he returned from serving Laban, and buried there the idols his family had brought with them (see Gn 35:4); and Shechem, situated in the valley between Mount Ebal and Mount Gerizim, was very likely the place where, right after the victory at Ai, Joshua had asked all the people to renew their commitment to the Law (see Jos 8:30-35).

On this visit he again asked the people to cling to the living and the true God. He knew that there was no such thing as a once-and-for-all decision to follow the Lord. Such decisions have to be reaffirmed by the older generation and accepted by the new. Joshua poured out his soul to all who listened.

The high point of his address comes in 24:14-15:

Now, therefore, fear the Lord and serve Him in sincerity and truth; and put away the gods which your fathers served beyond the River and in Egypt, and serve the Lord. And if it is disagreeable in your sight to serve the Lord, choose for yourselves today whom you will serve: whether the gods which your fathers served which were beyond the River, or the gods of the Amorites in whose land you are living; but as for me and my house, we will serve the Lord.

Some things in life are optional; you can choose where you live, you can choose your vocation or the car you drive. But other decisions are forced on us. Joshua said there were some choices that must be made by every living human being. And each of us must live with the consequences of our choices.

We Must Choose Our God

No person can live without a god. Joshua told the people they could choose pagan gods, such as the gods of Egypt or of the Canaanites in whose land they were dwelling. Or they could choose the Lord Jehovah. But choose they must!

Please notice: There is only one true God, but a multitude of pagan gods. Just as the pagans in the past were polytheists (believing in many gods), so today there are many idols that vie for our allegiance.

Though it is possible to serve many pagan gods, it is not possible to combine such worship with allegiance to the true and living God. Jehovah is a jealous God who will not share His glory with another. "No one can serve two masters" (Mt 6:24). It's like being married to two women at the same time, professing to love them equally. Those who claim to serve with a divided heart are actually serving an idol with their whole heart.

If Joshua were speaking today, he would challenge us to forsake the gods of contemporary society: money, sensual pleasure, and self-absorption. These are the gods that bid for our souls. They can be summarized by the phrase "self-will." That means simply, "I do what I want to do, and I believe what I want to believe."

And how can we identify our god? Just ask yourself two questions. First, what have I been thinking about the most this past week? Our minds home in on our god like a magnet.

Second, whom do I wish to please? Such questions will reveal the idolatry that is rampant within our own hearts. To repent of false worship should be our highest priority.

Someone has written:

The dearest idols I have known,
What e'er those idols be,
Help me to tear them from the throne,
And worship only Thee.

To tear the idols from our hearts is the most difficult spiritual act we will ever be called on to perform. It is also the most rewarding. For where God rules supreme there is freedom and strength.

God does not tolerate competition, for no other god is worthy to be compared with Him.

We Must Serve Our God

There is no god on earth or in heaven who does not demand allegiance. We may think that the false gods of the Egyptians or the Canaanites made no demands on their subjects. Not so! These gods expected not only worship but also sacrifice. Because of their demand for blood, the pagans would sacrifice their children to these deities. The people became victimized by the sensual appetites of the flesh and spirit involved in their pagan worship.

It was because of the very real power of these gods and the demonic forces behind them that the Lord commanded Joshua and the people to have no association with the nations of Canaan. The Israelites were to obey the Word of God, refusing the temptation to turn to the left or to the right, "in order that you may not associate with these nations, these which remain among you, or mention the name of their gods, or make anyone swear by them, or serve them, or bow down to them. But you are to cling to the Lord your God, as you have done to this day" (Jos 23:7-8).

When we choose Jehovah, we will not only serve Him but hate what He hates and love what He loves. For example, Christ taught that we should love our enemies so that "you will be sons of the Most High; for He Himself is kind to ungrateful and evil men" (Lk 6:35). To be godly is to be "godlike."

We become like the god we serve. Choose the god of greed, and you will end up lying and cheating to meet the demands of that god. Choose the god of sensuality and self-indulgence, and you will soon find yourself under the control of these pleasures. That's why Paul says, "Do you not know that when you present yourselves to someone as slaves for obedience, you are slaves of the one whom you obey, either of sin resulting in death, or of obedience resulting in righteousness?" (Rom 6:16).

"Paul, a bond-servant of Christ Jesus, called as an apostle, set apart for the gospel of God" (Rom 1:1). The question is not whether or not we will be slaves, but rather, whose slaves are we?

In her book *Smoke on the Mountain,* Joy Davidson asks a penetrating question: What is the shape of our idol? We can paraphrase her remarks by asking: Is your idol in the shape of a car, a house, clothes, membership in a club? She describes someone as saying, "I worship the pictures I paint, brother.... I worship my job.... I worship my golf game.... I worship my comfort; after all, isn't enjoyment the goal of life? I worship my church; I want to tell you, the work we've done in missions beats all other denominations in this city, and next year we can afford that new organ, and you won't find a better choir anywhere..." (The Westminster Press, 30-31; quoted in *Joshua,* Donald K. Campbell, Victor, 1981).

Our idol can have an external shape or it can simply be a conception of the mind. Whatever commands our allegiance and sustained attention is our god.

We Influence Others by Our Choice

Joshua ended his sermon by being an example of moral leadership: "As for me and my house, we will serve the Lord." When we choose our God others are influenced by our choice. Yes, it may be especially true that fathers influence their households, but everyone, children as well as adults, can have an influence. God only knows the full power of one person's uncompromising example.

Joshua not only influenced his own household but also motivated many others to serve the Lord. For good or for ill, our influence always extends beyond our immediate surroundings.

Aesop, you will recall, told a fable about an old crow who

was out in the wilderness and was very thirsty. He came to a jug that had a little water in the bottom of it. The old crow reached his beak into the jug to get some of that water, but his beak wouldn't quite touch the water. So he started picking up pebbles one at a time and dropping them into the jug, and soon the water rose in the jug until finally the crow was able to drink all that he desired.

As each of us drops our own little pebble into the common jug—teaching, showing hospitality, taking time to listen to a hurting friend—the water level rises high enough so that all are able to drink.

Joshua finished his speech, and the people made a covenant that they would serve the Lord their God. He then dismissed them to their inheritance. With that completed, we read, "And it came about after these things that Joshua the son of Nun, the servant of the Lord, died, being one hundred and ten years old" (Jos 24:29).

Joshua provided the fearless leadership needed by a nation which had come to believe that it was nothing but a swarm of grasshoppers. His challenge, like ours today, was to get the people to focus on God and not on themselves.

The difference between a grasshopper and a giant is only one of perspective. In dependence on God grasshoppers become giants and giant enemies become like grasshoppers. For as Isaiah says, all of us are grasshoppers in the presence of the Almighty: "It is He who sits above the vault of the earth, and its inhabitants are like grasshoppers, who stretches out the heavens like a curtain and spreads them out like a tent to dwell in" (Is 40:22).

Giants are grasshoppers who have seen themselves through the eyes of the living God.

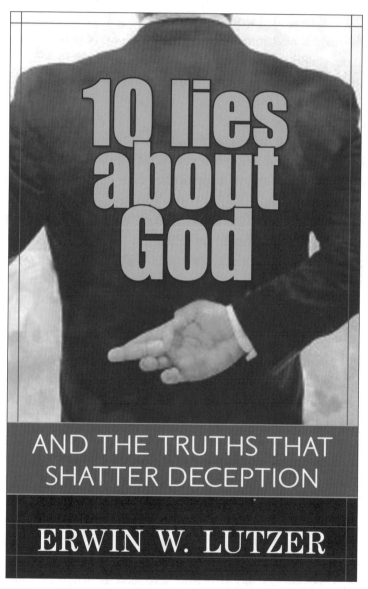

10 lies about God

AND THE TRUTHS THAT SHATTER DECEPTION

ERWIN W. LUTZER

ISBN: 978-0-8254-2945-3

Erwin Lutzer

THE
DOCTRINES
THAT
DIVIDE

A Fresh Look at the
Historic Doctrines That
Separate Christians

ISBN: 978-0-8254-3165-4

PASTOR
TO
PASTOR

Tackling the
Problems of
Ministry

Erwin Lutzer

ISBN: 978-0-8254-2947-7